# Understanding the Mysteries of Human Behavior

**Mark Leary, Ph.D.**

THE
GREAT
COURSES®

PUBLISHED BY:

**THE GREAT COURSES**
**Corporate Headquarters**
**4840 Westfields Boulevard, Suite 500**
**Chantilly, Virginia 20151-2299**
**Phone: 1-800-832-2412**
**Fax: 703-378-3819**
**www.thegreatcourses.com**

# Mark Leary, Ph.D.
Garonzik Family Professor
of Psychology and Neuroscience
Duke University

Professor Mark Leary is Garonzik Family Professor of Psychology and Neuroscience at Duke University, where he heads the program in Social Psychology and is faculty director of the Duke Interdisciplinary Initiative in Social Psychology. He earned his bachelor's degree in Psychology from West Virginia Wesleyan College and his master's and doctoral degrees in Social Psychology from the University of Florida. He has taught previously at Denison University, The University of Texas at Austin, and Wake Forest University, where he served as department chair.

Professor Leary has published 12 books and more than 200 scholarly chapters and articles on topics dealing with social motivation and emotion and the negative effects of excessive egotism and self-focus. He has been particularly interested in the ways in which people's emotions, behaviors, and self-views are influenced by their concerns with other people's perceptions and evaluations of them.

Professor Leary's books include *Social Anxiety*; *Self-Presentation: Impression Management and Interpersonal Behavior*; *The Curse of the Self: Self-Awareness, Egotism, and the Quality of Human Life*; *Handbook of Self and Identity*; and *Introduction to Behavioral Research Methods*. Based on his scholarly contributions, the *Personality and Social Psychology Bulletin* designated him among the top 40 social and personality psychologists in the world with the greatest impact. In 2010, he received the Lifetime Career Award from the International Society for Self and Identity. In addition, he was the founding editor of the journal *Self and Identity* and is currently the editor of *Personality and Social Psychology Review*. He is a fellow of the Association for Psychological Science, the American Psychological Association, and the Society for Personality and Social Psychology. ■

# Table of Contents

# Table of Contents

# Table of Contents

# Understanding the Mysteries of Human Behavior

**Scope**:

Human beings are puzzling creatures. We are capable of the most magnificent personal and cultural accomplishments, yet we sometimes behave in ways that are not only irrational and short sighted, but that also harm ourselves or others. We can experience uplifting emotions such as love, optimism, and awe, yet we also tie ourselves in knots of anxiety, anger, and despair. We sometimes stand up for our principles, but at other times, we behave contrary to our personal standards. We can remember thousands of trivial facts but forget an important appointment.

This set of 24 lectures examines some particularly puzzling aspects of human nature—features of people's thoughts, emotions, and behaviors that have intrigued scientists and laypeople alike. Relying on the latest theories and research from psychology, neuroscience, and other behavioral sciences, each lecture in this course addresses a provocative question about human behavior.

After an introductory lecture that sets the stage for the course, the lectures examine what is known about provocative phenomena such as dreaming, memory and forgetting, blushing, lapses of self-control, self-esteem, stress, risk taking, negative emotions, personality development, unconscious processes, happiness, differences between men and women, conflict and aggression, love, and the highly controversial question of whether some people have psychic abilities. The final lecture examines some phenomena that remain particularly poorly understood, including laughter, art, and consciousness.

In some instances, you'll find that researchers have a pretty firm grasp of the causes of the puzzling behavior of humans, and the lecture will offer a reasonably confident explanation of the phenomenon in question. However, in other cases, even after discovering what research has revealed about the topic, you'll be left with lingering questions. You'll also find that this is the nature of science—each answer arising from research comes with a new set of questions trailing behind it.

Along the way, you'll learn that certain puzzling features of human behavior can be traced to our evolutionary history. Modern humans show behavioral and emotional tendencies that would have promoted the survival and reproduction of prehistoric ancestors, even though those patterns are no longer useful—and may even be harmful—in modern times. You will also find that a good deal of your behavior and emotion is influenced by the ways that you talk to yourself in your own mind. Self-awareness is a cardinal human characteristic, and certain enigmatic behaviors make sense once you understand how people think about themselves and their situation. You'll also learn how cultural factors influence behavior; none of us can fully appreciate the degree to which we are influenced by aspects of the culture in which we have been raised.

You'll learn that people are often not aware of the factors that cause them to behave in particular ways or to experience particular emotions. Sometimes the important causes of behavior are outside of awareness, but at other times, people are simply mistaken about what causes them to feel or act in a certain way. However, well-designed research can often reveal the underlying causes.

As the lectures address the many mysteries of human behavior, you'll learn about how behavioral scientists study these phenomena and why certain questions about thought, emotion, and behavior have been particularly difficult to answer using scientific methods. You'll also discover that many popular and widely held explanations for various human behaviors are, at best, terribly incomplete or, at worst, completely incorrect.

While addressing various mysteries of human behaviors, the lectures also delve into how these puzzling behaviors relate to an array of interesting topics, such as overeating, fear, road rage, marriage and divorce, disgust, charisma, sexuality, child rearing, political attitudes, mental illness, bad habits, advertising, poverty and wealth, motivation, and other important aspects of people's lives.

Drawing upon the latest research in the behavioral sciences, this course shines a light into the deepest parts of the human mind, giving us profound insights into why we do what we do and revealing the fascinating side of seemingly ordinary human behaviors. ∎

# Solving Psychological Mysteries
## Lecture 1

This course will explore the latest theories and research from psychology and other behavioral sciences in order to try to understand a variety of rather ordinary, but often quite puzzling, aspects of human behavior—such as happiness, conflict, blushing, love, dreaming, memory, stress, and self-esteem. This first lecture will introduce the broad themes—evolution, self-awareness, and culture—that are going to help explain various mysteries of human behavior. Additionally, these themes will be applied to a mystery that involves the provocative differences between men and women.

**Human Behavior**
- People have been interested in questions about human behavior at least since the beginning of recorded history. Before the emergence of scientific methods, however, early thinkers couldn't test their ideas the way modern behavioral scientists can.

- During the latter part of the 1800s, learned people began to realize that they could answer questions about behavior—such as emotion, motivation, memory, personality, and intelligence—using the same kinds of scientific thinking that were already successful in sciences such as biology, chemistry, and physics.

- In modern times, the work of a few creative scientists has blossomed into a very large enterprise, involving hundreds of thousands of researchers around the world who study behavior and psychological processes.

- Although biological research supports the idea that human beings evolved through natural selection, many people have a hard time viewing human beings as just another species. Human beings are unusual animals, and many of the answers to puzzling aspects of human behavior lie in understanding some basic things about human beings.

- There are three broad themes that will follow us through our investigation into the mysteries of human behavior: evolution, self-awareness, and culture.

**Evolution**

- Like all life on Earth, human beings have evolved through a process of natural selection that turned us into the kind of animal that we are.

- Evolution is important to understanding certain mysteries of human behavior because, in some cases, a behavior that is difficult to understand in modern times makes sense when we consider the possibility that the puzzling behavior evolved to deal with a particular problem that our ancestors faced during the distant evolutionary past.

- For example, many people experience a fear of heights when they look out of a tall building. This seems to be completely irrational—and it is—but for millions of years, when people looked down from a very high place, they were probably up in a tree or at the edge of a cliff and had every reason to be nervous and careful. In fact, those individuals who were not nervous were often careless and didn't survive. Therefore, we are the descendants of people who were uneasy and cautious in high places.

**Self-Awareness**

- The uniquely human capacity for abstract **self-awareness**—our ability to think consciously about ourselves—is the single psychological characteristic that most clearly distinguishes human beings from all other animals.

- All animals can think—in the sense that their brains process information about themselves and their environments—but research suggests that only a few species can think consciously about themselves, and no other animal can think consciously about itself in the complex and abstract ways that we can.

© iStockphoto/Thinkstock.

**The fear of heights that many people experience seems irrational, but it does have an evolutionary basis.**

- For example, the ability to plan ahead is an important feature of the human mind because much of what people do each day is in the service of their long-term goals. If people didn't have the ability to think consciously about themselves, they couldn't think ahead. Only a few other animals are able to plan for the near future, but they are not able to plan for the long term because they can't imagine themselves in the distant future in their own minds.

- Self-awareness also allows people to think about who they are and what they are like, to evaluate themselves, and even to change their behavior if they don't like something about themselves. The ability to even try to purposefully change oneself is a uniquely human ability.

- Certain other animals—particularly the great apes and dolphins— do have a rudimentary ability to think about themselves. We know this because of research that has studied these animals' recognition of and reaction to their own reflections.

- Of course, we can think about ourselves in much more abstract and complex ways than other animals can. This ability to think consciously about ourselves is important in understanding human behavior; certain puzzling behaviors occur because of the ways that people think about and talk to themselves in their own minds.

## Culture
- A third theme that will be critical throughout this course relates to **culture**—all of the socially transmitted beliefs and behavior patterns in a group or society. Culture helps to make us different from other animals because it allows new ideas and techniques to be passed from generation to generation. In this way, culture allows human accomplishments to be cumulative.

- Scientists once believed that no other animal shows any indication of culture, but we now know that that's not true. No other species has the elaborate beliefs, rituals, and customs that human cultures have, but certain other animals can pass along behavior patterns to other group members that then persist over time.

- Culture is important in understanding certain puzzling behaviors because people often do odd things because that's what their culture says that they should do. Something that seems bizarre when viewed through the eyes of one culture or subculture may make perfect sense when we look at it through the eyes of another.

## Mysteries of Human Behavior
- Human behavior is exceptionally complicated at times, being influenced by many interacting forces. Some of the causes of behavior lie in the genetic blueprint that designed our brains, but much of behavior is influenced by people's personal experiences— by how they were raised and by the influence of other people, social groups, and culture. In trying to understand behavior, psychological scientists struggle to make sense of all that complexity in research studies that can tackle only a limited number of variables at a time.

- Although it's relatively easy for researchers to design studies in which they measure many variables and analyze the relationships among them, those kinds of studies usually don't provide definitive evidence about the causes of puzzling behaviors. The problem is that even when we find that variables are related to each other, we often can't identify which variables actually cause people's reactions.

- To understand the causes of behavior, researchers must conduct controlled experiments. However, many topics are difficult, if not impossible, to study under controlled conditions. For example, we can't conduct controlled experiments on the causes of phenomena such as child abuse, depression, or alcoholism because we would have to subject people to conditions that might cause them to abuse their children, become depressed, or develop a drinking problem.

- Ethical and methodological constraints on the kinds of research that scientists can conduct limit the strength of the conclusions that they can draw. As a result, scientists conduct the best research they can, knowing that they may often have only a piece of the puzzle at the end.

**Men versus Women: A Psychological Mystery**
- Nine out of 10 prison inmates are men; among people who are homeless, men outnumber women by at least three to one; men are 10 times more likely to commit murder than women are; men are more likely to show up at the low end of distributions of IQ scores—they are more likely to be mentally retarded—than women; and men are more likely to abuse and abandon their children and less likely to take care of their aging parents than women.

- On psychological measures of undesirable characteristics, men outscore women on measures of cruelty, closed-mindedness, hostility, narcissism, and self-indulgence. Additionally, men die earlier than women—about five years earlier on average.

- This is a particularly puzzling picture, given that we normally assume that men in most societies have it better than women do. Why would the advantaged gender be so much more maladjusted, antisocial, and unhealthy? This is an extremely complex issue, and the experts don't agree on its answer.

- First, there may be some evolutionary and biological processes at play. These differences between men and women can be seen around the world, and they don't map easily onto cultural variables.

- Furthermore, there's evidence that, for some reason, evolution operated in such a way that men show greater variability on many characteristics than women do—more men score at the extremes of distributions than women do.

- On average, men are taller than women, but men show more variability around the average height than women do. We also see this effect for birth weight. Height and weight are important examples because they are determined mostly by people's genes.

- Biologists disagree about why this occurs, but the phenomenon appears to be real. This extra variability might explain—at least in part—why men are more likely to have behavioral and social problems than women because the fact that men are more variable than women may naturally lead more men to have problems.

- Culture might also contribute to the high proportion of men who have serious problems. Throughout history, men have been expected to go to war in service to their country—even though there are more women entering the military than ever before. Many of the men with serious dysfunctions are veterans who have experienced psychological problems, have developed addictions, or have become homeless.

- According to U.S. Department of Labor statistics, 92 percent of Americans who die on the job are men. This is perhaps because men are more likely than women to work in dangerous jobs—which is exceptionally stressful—and perhaps those stressors contribute to some of the differences between men and women.

- Men are overrepresented in these jobs because, in some cases, it may be due to size or strength—but often it is due to cultural norms. Men are also more likely to be raised to think of themselves in these kinds of occupations.

- The fact that people can think consciously about themselves, including their gender and society's expectations for them, helps to lead men down some of the roads that end in psychological problems. It's partly a matter of differences in men's and women's self-images.

- Of course, women have their own sets of psychological problems— they are more likely to become depressed, for example—but men specialize in antisocial, self-destructive, and aggressive kinds of problems.

- Researchers can document the factors that are associated with these differences between men and women, but there's no easy way to identify precisely what causes them because we can't do controlled experiments to identify the causes of alcoholism, homelessness, child abuse, or murder.

- Behavioral scientists have made great progress in understanding differences between men and women, but the inherent complexity of human behavior means that some mysteries are very difficult to crack.

**culture**: All of the socially transmitted beliefs and behavior patterns in a group or society.

**self-awareness**: The human ability to think consciously about oneself.

Baumeister, *Is There Anything Good about Men?*

Hock, *Forty Studies That Changed Psychology.*

1. In what ways is the human ability to be self-aware responsible for many of the differences that we see between human beings and other animals?

2. What are some reasons that men may be more likely than women to show serious social and personal problems—such as violence, criminality, and homelessness?

# How Did Human Nature Evolve?
## Lecture 2

Understanding the process of evolution is important for uncovering certain mysteries of human behavior because in some cases, the answer to the puzzle has to do with how human nature evolved. Evolutionary psychologists have found consistencies in what most people strive for in their daily lives, and they have concluded that many psychological characteristics—such as fear, aggression, and overeating—evolved in the same way that physical characteristics evolved. Knowing that we're working against millions of years of evolution helps us understand why human nature sometimes leads us to behave in ways that aren't always in our best interests.

### Personality and Human Nature

- In psychology, **personality** refers to consistencies in a person's behavior across various situations and over time—the ways in which a person generally tends to respond.

- When we look at people's emotions and behaviors, we find that some consistent patterns are shared by almost everybody, but other patterns of consistency differ across people. To understand the puzzle of personality, we need to examine both consistencies that are shared by almost everybody—human nature—as well as consistencies that are seen in some people, but not in others—what psychologists call individual differences.

- When most people think of evolution, they usually think of how animals' physical characteristics evolved through natural selection; most people don't think about the role that evolutionary processes played in the development of behavioral and psychological characteristics.

- Charles Darwin recognized that his theory of natural selection applied not only to the evolution of physical characteristics but also to behavioral and emotional reactions. Darwin also knew that many people had more difficulty accepting his ideas when he applied them to people than when he talked about other animals, so he mostly confined himself to explaining the behaviors of animals other than human beings.

For humans, the problem of overeating evolved from having to forage for food and not having a place to store it.

- During the late 1800s, many psychologists began to apply evolutionary thinking to understanding human behavior, but then they dropped the idea of evolution—even while biology was rebuilding itself around evolutionary ideas.

- The main reason was that mainline scientific psychology became dominated by radical **behaviorism**, which was based on the idea that all behaviors, as well as all emotional responses, are the result of learning. According to behaviorism, people do what they do and feel what they feel because they have been conditioned to respond in certain ways.

- Behaviorism dominated scientific psychology during much of the 20th century. It wasn't until the 1980s that evolutionary ideas started creeping back into psychology. By the 1990s, a new subspecialty known as **evolutionary psychology** had emerged that focused specifically on the evolutionary underpinnings of human behavior.

- During the long span of human evolution, our prehistoric ancestors faced some recurring challenges and problems that had implications for their survival and reproduction—such as finding food, protecting

13

themselves, and managing social relationships. Some individuals had characteristics that helped them meet these adaptive challenges more successfully than other individuals. The individuals who had these helpful characteristics were more successful in producing offspring and transmitting their genes to future generations than those who did not tend to respond as adaptively.

- As a result, individuals who survived and reproduced successfully passed their genes along at a higher rate, including genes that were associated with those behaviors that helped them meet those life challenges successfully. Individuals that did not survive or reproduce as successfully did not pass along their genes at the same rate, so genes that were associated with less adaptive patterns of behavior decreased in the species over time.

- Therefore, we are the descendants of those individuals throughout evolutionary history who were most successful at surviving and reproducing. If all members of a species share a particular characteristic, one explanation is that the characteristic was adaptive for generation after generation of our ancestors.

- One primary place where evolution seems to have played a role is in people's motives and goals. Evolutionary psychologists have concluded that across cultures, humans are motivated by a need for social acceptance, a desire to belong to groups, a need to influence other people, a tendency to protect ourselves against people who might harm us, and a strong inclination to establish intimate relationships.

- These five motives are central to human nature; more specific goals are often in the service of these five broader motives. We simply don't find otherwise normal, well-adjusted people who have the opposite motives.

- Human nature consistently emphasizes these basic motives because these are motives that would have promoted survival and reproduction during the evolutionary past. Individuals who weren't motivated to do these things—or worse, wanted to do the opposite—didn't fare as well. Therefore, you are motivated to do much of what you do every day because evolution built those motives into human nature.

## Evolutionary Adaptation: Fear

- One of the topics to which Darwin applied evolutionary ideas was the topic of emotions, which also evolved because they provided an adaptive benefit for our ancestors.

- For example, fear alerts us to dangers and leads us to avoid things that might hurt us. Of course, people can learn to be afraid of things that don't pose any real danger, but fear is fundamentally related to the human motive to protect ourselves.

- Fears that are largely universal—the things that human beings tend to be afraid of without much learning—probably evolved. For example, our prehistoric ancestors who were afraid of snakes, which were a real threat, were much more likely to survive and reproduce than those who weren't afraid of snakes. Because we descended from individuals who were afraid of snakes, anxiety about snakes appears to be part of human nature.

- The same is true of how people react to spiders and snarling animals. Many people have negative reactions when they see even pictures or movies of snakes, spiders, or snarling animals because during evolutionary history, anytime you saw one of these creatures, it was really there. Your brain isn't designed to distinguish automatically between real threats and pictured threats.

- All animals, including human beings, are far more likely to overreact to something that's not actually threatening than they are to underreact, or not react at all, to a real threat. This overreaction to possible harm is also an evolved feature of the brain.

- Evolution seems to operate on the idea that it's better to experience unnecessary fear and to react as if something is dangerous when it's not than to fail to react to a real threat. Animals with very sensitive threat-detection systems were more likely to survive and reproduce, so that became a part of human nature, making us more reactive than we often need to be.

## Evolutionary Adaptation: Aggression

- Human beings are a very aggressive species, and even for those of us who don't actually harm other people, most of us occasionally have aggressive urges that we suppress.

- Most aggression seems pointless. Countries go to war over rather minor disputes, and people kill others over very minor slights; it often does not take much to unleash a violent episode. The tendency to aggress is built into the human psyche.

- According to evolutionary thinking, many instances of modern-day aggression are manifestations of strategies that facilitated survival and reproduction during evolutionary history. Aggression helps animals protect their territory, defend themselves and their offspring, and obtain and protect resources such as food.

- The same is true of human beings. In the days before we had culture, law enforcement, and armies to protect us, each person had to be able to fend off threats with aggression when necessary. Nonaggressive individuals simply would not have survived at the same rate, and their offspring would have been at risk as well.

- In modern civilizations, personal aggression is rarely helpful—in fact, it can get a person into a lot of trouble—but features of human nature evolved because they were adaptive in the environment in which our prehistoric ancestors lived during human evolution, and they may or may not make sense in the environments in which we live today.

- Human nature evolved mostly on the plains of Africa, where our ancestors wandered around as nomadic scavengers, gatherers, and hunters—long before there were settled communities. However, biologists largely agree that our brains have not changed much, if at all, in the short span of time that human beings have been living in civilized communities. This helps to explain behaviors that are part of human nature but that are not beneficial to many people today.

- In modern society, outbursts of deadly aggression are rarely beneficial to anyone, but before culture, police forces, and a judicial system, individuals who were willing to resort to lethal aggression to defend themselves, their food, their offspring, their clan, and their territory were more likely to survive—and to have offspring who survived—than individuals who were not aggressive. A willingness to resort to aggression was essential.

## Evolutionary Adaptation: Overeating

- Human beings have an evolved mechanism to eat whenever food is available. During virtually all of human evolution, our days were spent looking for food, and when we found some, it made sense to eat as much as possible because we had no way to store or carry extra food, and we didn't know how long it might be until we would eat again.

- The problem is that, in developed countries, most people now have much more food available than they need. In addition, we seem to have a particular penchant for sweet and fatty foods. This may be because foods like lettuce, celery, and tomatoes were fairly common on the plains of Africa, so there wasn't any benefit in being a glutton when it came to vegetables. However, sweet fruits and fatty animal flesh were less common.

- Many people react negatively to evolutionary explanations of behavior because they think that if some behavior, such as aggression or overeating, is natural, then it seems like we can't change it or maybe shouldn't even try—but that's not the case.

- These reactions were natural in the environment in which evolution occurred, but that doesn't mean that modern human beings should necessarily act in these ways. None of us are living naturally according to our evolved urges, and just because human nature was designed a certain way to meet the challenges of prehistoric life doesn't mean that we can't consciously decide to behave otherwise.

- Controlling a particular reaction is more difficult if it involves an evolutionary-designed system, but that simply means that we have to try harder—not that we shouldn't try at all. We can control our eating within limits, manage our aggressive impulses, and even make ourselves pick up a snake.

## Important Terms

**behaviorism**: A branch of psychology that claims that all behaviors and emotional responses are the result of learning.

**evolutionary psychology**: A branch of psychology that focuses specifically on the evolutionary underpinnings of human behavior.

**personality**: Consistencies in a person's behavior across various situations and over time.

## Suggested Reading

Buss, *Evolutionary Psychology.*

Pinker, *How the Mind Works.*

## Questions to Consider

1. According to evolutionary theory, what processes led human nature to take the form that it did?

2. What basic human motives that influence our behavior today appear to have been a product of natural selection?

# Where Do People's Personalities Come From?
## Lecture 3

Both nature and nurture—that is, both genetic and environmental influences—play a role in why people differ from one another. Heritability is a measure of how much of the variability that exists in people's personalities is due to genetic factors. Some personality traits and behaviors are directly caused by genetic influences on the brain, but others are caused indirectly, as a result of the complex ways that our genes shape and change our behavior and our environments. However, the precise biological mechanisms, the complex processes by which genes influence behavior, remain a mystery.

### Individual Differences in Personality

- Researchers in the field of personality psychology have been trying to figure out why people's personalities turn out differently for many years. Behavioral scientists have made great strides in this area, but the processes are so complex that we still have many unanswered questions.

- For many years, the question of individual differences was framed very simplistically as the **nature-nurture debate**: Is personality due mostly to nature—what you were born with—or is it due mostly to nurture—how you were raised?

- Science has swung back and forth on the answer to the nature-nurture debate over the years. In the first half of the 20th century, the widely accepted answer among psychologists was that most differences among people are learned—that they're due to nurture. The idea that people are born as a blank slate and gain their personalities through experience and learning was propagated by John Watson, the founder of behaviorism, and dominated American psychology for many years.

- However, as researchers dug more deeply into the nature of personality, they came to the conclusion that Watson was wrong. Personality is certainly influenced by people's personal experiences, but personality is also undoubtedly influenced by people's inborn biological makeup.

- The scientific field that studies the question of where differences in personality come from is known as **behavioral genetics**. Researchers in behavioral genetics are interested in both genetic and environmental influences on personality—as well as the interplay between them.

- More than 99 percent of every person's genes are identical to every other person's. In fact, we share about 98 percent of our genes with chimpanzees, our closest relative in the animal kingdom. The less than one percent of genes that are different from other people are the genes that make each of us look and act differently.

- Researchers look at how much certain personality characteristics—such as extroversion, stubbornness, or gullibility—are affected by genetics in general across all people and determine how much of the variability that they observe across people is due to genetic versus environmental factors.

### Heritability

- Behavior geneticists express the degree to which a personality trait is influenced by genes with a statistic called **heritability**, which tells us the proportion of the observed variability in a group of individuals that can be accounted for by genetic factors.

- Geneticists define heritability as the proportion of **phenotypic variance**—the variability that we observe in a trait or characteristic—that is attributable to **genotypic variance**, which is the variability in people's genes. Heritability, therefore, is the proportion of the total variability that we observe in a characteristic that's due to variability in genes.

- Measures of heritability are just estimates. When a characteristic has a heritability above zero, we know that genetic influences are operating, but we can't always specify exactly how large that influence is because it depends on the group that we're studying. Of course, if we get about the same heritability estimate no matter which group we test, then we can be more confident of the precise value.

### Determining Heritability: Twins

- Many of the methods that researchers use to determine the heritability of a personality characteristic are based on comparisons of the personalities of twins, which come in two varieties: identical, or monozygotic, twins and fraternal, or dizygotic, twins.

- Monozygotic twins are perfectly genetically identical because they came from the same fertilized egg. In contrast, dizygotic twins share only 50 percent of their genes—just like ordinary brothers and sisters do. By comparing the personalities of pairs of monozygotic and dizygotic twins, researchers can estimate the heritability of personality characteristics.

- Researchers are particularly interested in comparing twins who were raised together by the same parents to twins who were raised separately by different families. By comparing twins who were raised together to twins who were raised apart, we can more cleanly separate genetic from environmental influences on personality.

- If identical twins who were raised by different families since birth have similar personalities, then those similarities are probably due to the fact that they have the same genes—because the environments in which they were raised were different.

- Extroversion and neuroticism are the two most important personality traits because as we look at differences among people, how extroverted and neurotic people are relate more strongly to their behaviors than any other personality traits.

- **Extroversion** involves the degree to which people are talkative and sociable. People who score high in extroversion are outgoing, enjoy interacting with other people, and seek out stimulating activities. People who are low in extroversion—**introverts**—are quiet, less outgoing, and sometimes shy.

- Research on tens of thousands of twins shows that, depending on the group studied, the heritability of extroversion is somewhere in the vicinity of 0.5 to 0.6, which means that about 50 percent of the variability that we observe in how extroverted versus introverted people are is due to genetic factors.

- **Neuroticism** involves how much people experience negative emotions. People high in neuroticism tend to be more moody, emotional, anxious, and prone to stress than people who are low in neuroticism, who show greater emotional stability.

- Research shows that the heritability of neuroticism is somewhere in the range of 0.3 to 0.5, depending on the group studied. This means that when we look out and see differences in how emotionally stable versus emotionally volatile people are, a little less than half of those differences in neuroticism—30 to 50 percent—can be traced to genetic factors.

- One of the biggest surprises in behavioral genetics was the discovery that attitudes and values also have genetic underpinnings. Traditionally, psychologists have assumed that values and character traits—such as integrity and compassion—are instilled by parents, teachers, and religions. In part, they are, but there are also genetic influences.

**Direct Genetic Effects on Personality**
- Researchers estimate that traditional, conservative values and attitudes—for example, attitudes toward the death penalty, gay marriage, and censorship—have a heritability of 0.59. In other words, about 60 percent of the variability that we see in basic political attitudes has a genetic component. This could be explained

by the fact that liberal or conservative values are often rooted in aspects of personality that are partly genetically determined.

- Smoking and drinking are behaviors that are influenced by many factors, but genes play a role. There isn't a gene for smoking, but it's more likely that people with certain patterns of personality are more likely to smoke than people with other personalities.

- Research shows, for example, that people who are higher in extroversion are more likely to smoke—as are people who score higher in neuroticism. This makes sense because one of the strongest predictors of smoking is the degree to which people enjoy and seek out stimulating activities, and nicotine is a stimulant.

- If we look at all of the studies that have been conducted as a whole, the heritability for drinking alcohol is around 0.4. The heritability of

People that have an extroverted personality are outgoing and enjoy interacting with other people.

alcoholism is even higher—somewhere above 0.5. In other words, about 50 percent of the variability that we see in whether people have serious drinking problems has a genetic basis.

- Whether people get married—and whether they stay married—also have genetic underpinnings. A study at the University of Minnesota involving over 2,000 pairs of twins found that the heritability of marriage is 0.68.

- Genes also play a role in how well people's marriages go. For example, women who are optimistic, warm, and low in aggressiveness are happier with their marriages than women who are less optimistic, less warm, and more aggressive—and these characteristics are partly heritable. This may be because positive people will have more positive reactions to things that happen in their marriages.

- The likelihood of getting divorced is heritable as well, and the heritability of divorce is estimated to be between 0.3 and 0.4. Research suggests that much of this effect has to do with characteristics that involve negative emotionality.

- Overall, across the dozens of traits that have been studied, most personality characteristics have heritability coefficients between 0.2 and 0.5. What's being inherited is not a personality trait but, rather, the genes that influence your nervous system to respond in particular ways.

**Indirect Genetic Effects on Personality**
- In addition to the relatively direct effects of genes on people's behavior—in which genes create a brain that tends to respond in particular ways—genes can have indirect effects on personality by creating changes in people's environments.

- Each of us plays a role in creating our own environment and life situation, and genes are partly responsible for the choices that we make in life; our genes help to create our environment, and then that environment can influence our personality.

- Scientists call effects in which genes affect people's environments **gene-environment correlations**. An active gene-environment correlation is "active" because genes influence behavior in a way that leads people to seek out and construct certain situations, which then influence their personalities.

- For example, activity level is a highly heritable trait. Some babies are active while others are more sedate. As these babies get older, the more active ones are going to be more interested in running and playing while the children who are not as active might spend more time reading. You learn different things and develop different skills from playing sports than from reading, so the activities that children choose—activities that are influenced by their genes—change their personality.

- A reactive, or evocative, gene-environment correlation is "evocative" because genes influence the person's behavior in ways that evoke certain reactions from other people.

- For example, if a parent sees that a child really enjoys music but doesn't enjoy sports, the parent will be more likely to buy the child things that involve music rather than sports and encourage music lessons rather than team sports. Therefore, the child's genes foster behavior that lead parents to create a different environment, which then has downstream consequences for the child's personality.

- These effects of genes on people's social environment are cumulative. One initial genetic difference in a child's activity level or irritability can start a sequence of behaviors and events that cascade for the rest of the person's life, building on each other over time. Therefore, relatively small genetic differences at birth can become compounded year after year—and this process continues for people's entire lives.

- Part of the difficulty in understanding how personality develops is that the effects are complex—depending not only on many genes operating together and many kinds of environments in which children grow up, but also on interactions between genes and the environment.

## Important Terms

**behavioral genetics**: The scientific field that studies both the genetic and environmental influences on such characteristics as personality.

**extroversion**: The degree to which people are talkative and sociable.

**gene-environment correlation**: The effect in which genes affect people's environments.

**genotypic variance**: The variability in people's genes.

**heritability**: The proportion of the observed variability in a group of individuals that can be accounted for by genetic factors; the proportion of phenotypic variance that is attributable to genotypic variance.

**introversion**: The degree to which people are quiet and sometimes shy.

**nature-nurture debate**: The debate over whether people's personalities are due mostly to nature—what they were born with—or mostly to nurture—how they were raised.

**neuroticism**: The degree to which people experience negative emotions.

**phenotypic variance**: The variability that is observed in a trait or characteristic of people.

## Suggested Reading

de Waal, "The End of Nature versus Nurture."

Shaffer, *Social and Personality Development*.

## Questions to Consider

1. When behavioral geneticists calculate the heritability of a personality characteristic, what does the value of the heritability coefficient tell them?

2. In what ways do people's genes help to create the environments in which they live?

# How Can Siblings Be So Different?
## Lecture 4

The genes that people inherit from their parents help to build a brain that tends to operate in certain ways, leading to the idiosyncratic patterns of behavior that we call personality. The rest of the variability that we see in people's personalities is due to environmental or situational influences—mostly people's personal experiences and how they are treated by other people, including their parents, while they were growing up. Although we are often surprised when children from the same family turn out differently, once we understand the processes that are involved, it's not as much of a mystery as it first appears to be.

## Genetics and Siblings

- At the time of conception, the 23 chromosomes in the mother's egg and the 23 chromosomes in the father's sperm combine, resulting in a baby with 46 chromosomes. As a result, you share half of your genes with your mother and half of your genes with your father.

- If you have any siblings, your brothers and sisters also inherited 23 chromosomes from each of your parents. Therefore, on average, you share about half of your genes with each of your brothers and sisters. However, unless you have an identical twin, your brothers' and sisters' chromosomes have different combinations of genes than yours do.

- Changing just one gene in a sequence can change the genetic makeup of a person entirely. Therefore, although your sibling and you share roughly half of your genes, you don't share some of the sequences of genes that are responsible for complex aspects of your personalities. As a result, you don't appear to be as similar as people might expect based on the fact that you have half of your genes in common.

- Furthermore, identical twins are often much more than twice as similar as ordinary siblings or as dizygotic, or fraternal, twins are. In sharing 100 percent of their genes, identical twins also share all of the unique combinations of genes that normal siblings don't.

- One example of this phenomenon is known as **emergenesis**, which occurs when a trait is determined by a particular configuration of many genes that then leads a person to display a particular characteristic that we don't see in the rest of the person's family.

- One way that researchers can spot emergenic characteristics is when data shows that identical twins are very similar but that fraternal twins are not. It turns out that the correlations for a particular trait, such as extroversion, are very high for identical twins but low for fraternal twins. This pattern suggests that extroversion is emergenic; it's partly genetically determined but doesn't run strongly in families. Therefore, one dizygotic twin might be quite outgoing while the other might be quite introverted—even though they share 50 percent of their genes.

- A person's emotional tone is also somewhat emergenic. Having a really optimistic outlook, having control over one's emotions, staying cool under pressure, and having a high capacity for happiness seems to require a particular combination of genes. Siblings who are not twins can be quite different in their emotional tone, but identical twins tend to be much more similar in their emotionality.

- Behavioral geneticists suggest that special talents are often emergenic. Some researchers think that charisma is also a type of emergenic trait. Charisma requires many characteristics to align—including physical attractiveness, moderate extroversion, sociability, interpersonal skills, relatability, self-confidence, and good verbal ability.

- Charisma requires a combination of a high level of all these things, each of which has some genetic basis. If you don't have them all, you probably aren't highly charismatic. It's possible, then, for one child to have the right combination of genes and exude charisma while his or her sibling is rather dull and uninteresting.

- Although children in the same family share 50 percent of their genes, they don't share many of the gene combinations that underlie complex aspects of personality and ability. Brothers and sisters are sometimes not as similar as we intuitively expect because personality often depends on particular configurations of genes that brothers and sisters don't necessarily share.

## Environmental Influences on Personality

- Children who are raised by the same parents in the same way in the same environment don't necessarily turn out to be similar. It is certainly true that environmental influences, including parenting, affect personality. However, researchers have found that the environments that children from the same family share with each other exert a much weaker influence on their personalities than the environments that each child experiences individually.

- Research shows that shared experiences that are common to all children in a family affect their personalities far less than unshared environmental influences that each child experiences separately. Therefore, the common environments and experiences that children in a family share don't make them as similar to each other as we might expect.

- If a shared family environment made children similar to each other, then children with different biological parents who are adopted into the

Siblings share roughly half of their genes, but they don't appear as similar as we might expect.

29

same family should have personalities that are more similar than two unrelated children who grew up in different homes. According to the latest research, however, they're not.

- Additionally, when researchers analyze why identical twins are so similar psychologically, they find that the similarity is due almost entirely to genetics and not to the fact that they grew up in the same environment.

- **Shared influences** are things that are common to all children in a family—including the house and town they live in, the number of TV sets and books in the house, and their parents' attitudes and values.

- **Unshared influences** are things that children in the same family don't share. For example, the kids probably have different sets of friends and different teachers in school. Their parents probably treat them a bit differently as well—both because each child is different to begin with and because the parents themselves change as they have more children.

- Siblings in the same family have different personal experiences, illnesses, and injuries—and even world events may affect siblings differently, depending on how old they are at the time of these events. Therefore, even children growing up in the same family have many different, unshared experiences.

- In some studies, the shared environment exerts little or no discernible impact on personality. For example, once we control for the genetic similarity among brothers and sisters, they are barely any more similar to one another than randomly selected people—even though they grew up in the same family.

- Even when children grow up in the same home environment, the things that they experience in common do not cause their personalities to be similar. In other words, the critical childhood experiences that affect personality involve the unique experiences that children have. This effect has been shown many times in different kinds of studies on different populations by different investigators, so it appears to be a valid and robust finding.

## Unshared versus Shared Environments

- There are several reasons that unshared environments are more important than shared environments. First, we tend to overestimate how similar the environment is for children who grow up in the same family. As they get older, children spend more and more of their time in situations that don't involve their siblings. As a result, there are many more unshared experiences that cause them to be different.

- A second reason that shared environments exert relatively little influence on people's personalities is that exactly the same environment or experience might be perceived differently by different children. In addition, if the children perceive an objective event differently, it may affect them in quite different ways.

- For example, is divorce a shared or an unshared event for siblings? The answer depends on whether you're considering the objective event, which is shared, or the idiosyncratic impact of the event, which is unshared.

- Siblings may disagree about whether certain shared experiences were good or bad. Looking at your family experiences from the outside, an observer might think that you and your siblings shared many experiences, but you really didn't because your subjective experience of living in the small town or going to the beach, for example, was much different than theirs.

- Another reason that children growing up in the same family often turn out differently is that there are certain genes that influence behavior only when the person experiences a particular environmental event. In other words, whether you are affected by certain events and experiences depends on whether you have certain genes.

- For example, there are two forms of a gene that are related to the neurotransmitter serotonin. Under normal circumstances, people with these two forms of the gene—geneticists call them **alleles**—don't act differently. However, when they experience highly stressful life events, people with one form of the gene are likely to become depressed, but those with the other form of the gene don't become depressed.

- We have no idea how many genes have different effects depending on the environment, but behavioral geneticists assume that these gene-environment interactions are pretty common.

- There are certainly a few areas in which effects of the shared environment have been found, but they tend not to be personality traits but, rather, attitudes and beliefs. Children do tend to adopt the belief systems of their parents to some extent, and even if they reject their parents' beliefs later, those beliefs still have an effect at times.

- The fact that the shared family environment has little effect on the development of people's personalities has led some people to conclude that parents don't matter very much. They conclude that if the shared family environment is unrelated to children's personalities, then the parents must not make much of a difference in how their children turn out. However, this is not a valid conclusion.

- The research on shared and unshared environments doesn't show that parents don't have any effect on their kids; rather, it shows that parents don't have the same effect on all of their children.

- The fact is that parents don't treat all of their children the same. Many parents try, thinking that they should treat all of the children alike, but they really can't—and they probably shouldn't because each child is already different at the time they're born. Based on their individual genetic make-up, they have different traits, needs, and ways of reacting that parents respond to differently.

- Parents create different family environments for their children. They may have a great impact on all of their children, but their behavior as parents will often cause differences rather than similarities in the children's personalities. Additionally, children may respond differently to precisely the same parenting.

- What appears to be the same environment may be perceived differently by children with different personalities. The parents are affecting their children, but the children are reacting in different ways—which is another reason why children from the same family can be so different.

## Important Terms

**allele**: A different form of a gene.

**emergenesis**: Occurs when a trait is determined by a particular configuration of many genes that then leads a person to display a particular characteristic that is not seen in the rest of the person's family.

**shared influence**: An influence that is common to all children in a family.

**unshared influence**: An influence that children in the same family don't share.

## Suggested Reading

Rutter, *Genes and Behavior*.

Wright, *Twins*.

1. Discuss three reasons that children from the same family are not as similar as most people expect that they should be.

2. Why do the environments that children do not share with their brothers and sisters exert a stronger influence on their personalities than the environments that they do share?

# Why Do People Need Self-Esteem—Or Do They?
## Lecture 5

<br>

Researchers, practicing psychologists, parents, teachers, and many others believe that low self-esteem is associated with many serious personal and social problems and that increasing people's self-esteem will make them more successful, happier, well-adjusted people. In fact, some of the experts in the field have made very strong claims about the importance of self-esteem—such as the notion that virtually every psychological problem is due to low self-esteem. Other experts have suggested that increasing self-esteem not only helps people as individuals but can also solve social problems. In this lecture, you'll learn how sociometer theory helps unravel the mystery of self-esteem.

**High versus Low Self-Esteem**
- **Self-esteem** refers to how positively people feel about themselves. It is not the same as **self-confidence**, which is the belief that you can do certain things or bring about certain outcomes. Self-esteem is not a belief; it's a feeling or evaluation that people have about themselves.

- Psychologists distinguish between two forms of self-esteem: **Trait self-esteem** reflects how good you feel about yourself in general or on average, and **state self-esteem**, which involves how you feel about yourself at any particular moment in time. State self-esteem fluctuates as people go through their days.

- Research suggests that low self-esteem is associated with undesirable behaviors and emotions and that high self-esteem is associated with desirable behaviors and emotions. People who are higher in self-esteem are more likely to be happy with their lives and less likely to become depressed or be anxious or worried. People with high self-esteem do better in their jobs, tend to be better educated, and tend to make more money.

- In contrast, people who score lower in self-esteem tend to be more dishonest, are more likely to engage in criminal activities, and are more likely to join gangs. They tend to underachieve, and they are more likely to have failures of all kinds. Almost all psychological problems are more common among people with lower self-esteem.

- Based on years of research, however, low self-esteem does not appear to cause the negative outcomes that have been associated with it, and high self-esteem does not appear to cause the positive outcomes. Instead, self-esteem is usually the result of these outcomes. For example, low self-esteem doesn't cause depression; the life events that cause depression also tend to lower self-esteem.

- Contrary to the popular view, there's almost no evidence that self-esteem causes anything, and studies that have looked at changes in people's self-esteem over time show that self-esteem is the result of certain experiences and events—that behaving in positive and negative ways leads to changes in self-esteem.

## Sociometer Theory

- One approach that explains the function of self-esteem and how it relates to positive and negative outcomes in life is **sociometer theory**, which proposes that self-esteem is a gauge—an internal, psychological meter—that monitors the degree to which a person is being valued and accepted versus devalued and rejected by other people.

- Human beings are very social creatures. We not only live in groups and form relationships with other people, but being accepted by other people is very important to us. A desire for social acceptance seems to have evolved as a universal human need.

- Before modern civilization, when our ancestors were living as hunters and gatherers, having a supportive group of people around you was critically important: A person who was not accepted by anybody would have had a very difficult time surviving.

- Social acceptance doesn't often have life-or-death consequences in modern society, but many aspects of human nature evolved because they were adaptive in an environment that was entirely unlike the modern world. Our brains evolved in an environment in which social rejection could actually kill you.

- Because social acceptance was so important—and social rejection was so dangerous and damaging—human beings are highly attuned to the degree that other people accept and reject them.

- Self-esteem is part of the system that helps us monitor our social worlds for indications that we might be rejected and motivates us to make ourselves acceptable to other people. This system—the sociometer—monitors not only other people's reactions for indications of how they feel about us, but also our own behavior because we need to know when we're doing something—or even thinking about doing something—that might lead others to reject us.

- When we get indications that our value and acceptance in the view of other people are increasing, our state self-esteem also increases; we feel good about ourselves, and we continue to do whatever we're doing. However, if we get indications that our value is going down and that other people might reject us, our self-esteem drops; we feel badly about ourselves, and we start analyzing the situation and ourselves to figure out what to do.

- The sociometer monitors the social situation and our behavior and gives us information about our social acceptability. This information comes in the form of good or bad feelings about ourselves. However, self-esteem doesn't cause behavior directly.

- Dozens of research studies show that people's state self-esteem rises and falls as events occur that connote acceptance and rejection. Some people claim that their self-esteem is not affected by what other people think of them, but studies show that even these people show pronounced changes in state self-esteem when they are accepted and rejected.

- Research shows that how we feel about ourselves when we do something depends on how we think other people will evaluate us. That's because self-esteem is a gauge. Just as the gas gauge of a car moves up and down with how much gas is in the tank, your state self-esteem moves up and down with changes in perceived acceptance and rejection.

- People differ in how good they typically feel about themselves. As we go through our daily lives, we're not always getting feedback about how much people value and accept us; however, if you were asked how you feel about yourself at any given time, you could come up with an answer.

- If self-esteem is a gauge, then trait self-esteem is the resting point on the gauge when you're not getting any feedback about yourself. It's how good a person generally feels in the absence of any incoming feedback at the moment.

- The resting point of the sociometer is primarily determined by a person's history of experiencing acceptance and rejection. People who have had a history of mostly acceptance will have relatively high trait self-esteem because they feel generally acceptable. People who have experienced a history of neglect, disinterest, or rejection may have lower trait self-esteem because they don't feel quite as generally acceptable.

- People use information from both their state and trait self-esteem to help them decide how to respond in particular social situations. To respond to situations that involve the threat of rejection, people must have a sense of the likelihood that they will be accepted or rejected in that particular situation, and that information is conveyed to them by their state self-esteem—how they feel about themselves at the moment. They also need to have a sense of how acceptable they are in general, and that information is conveyed by their trait self-esteem.

## Self-Esteem and Social Problems

- Some observers have suggested that many of our social problems come from a shortage of self-esteem, but there's no shortage of self-esteem. In fact, far more people have high self-esteem than low self-esteem. Most people have moderate or high self-esteem, and very few people feel completely bad about themselves.

- Most people who obtain lower scores on measures of self-esteem that psychologists use don't have genuinely low self-esteem. They actually fall around the midpoint of the scale and usually have mixed or ambivalent feelings about themselves—in contrast with people who have high self-esteem, who feel mostly good about themselves. Individuals who have genuinely low self-esteem are rare, but they do exist.

**A person with a psychological disorder often has low self-esteem because others distance themselves from them.**

- The reason that most people have moderate to high self-esteem is that most people feel at least mildly acceptable. Most people recognize that they have some positive characteristics and that at least a few people value and accept them. That's enough to keep people's self-esteem from being low.

- People who feel inadequately accepted by other people experience a number of negative emotions such as sadness, anxiety, anger, loneliness, jealousy, and shame. People who feel rejected naturally experience negative emotions, and they also tend to have lower self-esteem. Therefore, low self-esteem is related to certain negative emotions—not because self-esteem causes the emotions, but because rejection simultaneously causes the negative emotions and makes self-esteem decrease.

- In addition, some emotional and behavioral problems are related to self-esteem because they precipitate rejection. For example, nearly every psychological disorder leads other people to devalue and distance themselves from the troubled person. When people are chronically aggressive or depressed, other people tend to pull back, so it's not surprising that people with psychological difficulties—whatever their cause—tend to have lower self-esteem.

- Another way in which low self-esteem is related to certain personal and social problems is that feeling inadequately valued or rejected increases people's desire to be accepted. Presumably, people prefer to gain acceptance in socially desirable ways, but when they don't think they can do that, people who feel inadequately valued may resort to extreme, and sometimes deviant or antisocial, ways of finding acceptance.

- Knowing about people's self-esteem can tell us about the degree to which they feel like they are socially acceptable, and if their self-esteem is relatively low, it tells us that we need to pay attention to how acceptable they feel.

- We might even want to do something about it—either to help them improve in ways that promote their social connections, or if they are simply viewing themselves too negatively, to help them see that they are, in fact, a perfectly acceptable person.

- What we don't want to do is to try to increase people's self-esteem artificially—to build them up and make them feel that they are more socially acceptable than they actually are. People function best when they have a realistic view of their strengths and weaknesses, and if we prop their self-esteem up artificially, not only will it not work in the long run, but it can also create new problems.

- People who view themselves more positively than they should become confused and angry when other people don't seem to recognize their wonderfulness, and they can become unmotivated to change themselves in areas in which they could afford to improve. In the worst case, we can create a narcissist with an overblown sense of their worth and importance.

- Trying to increase self-esteem without focusing on people's social acceptability won't help, either. If we want to tackle the problems that are associated with low self-esteem, we need to focus on the quality of people's social lives and the degree to which they have adequate, supportive social relationships rather than on just trying to change their self-esteem.

## Important Terms

**self-confidence**: The belief that you can do certain things or bring about certain outcomes.

**self-esteem**: How positively people feel about themselves.

**sociometer theory**: A theory that proposes that self-esteem is a gauge—an internal, psychological meter—that monitors the degree to which a person is being valued and accepted versus devalued and rejected by other people.

**state self-esteem**: A form of self-esteem that involves how you feel about yourself at any particular moment in time.

**trait self-esteem**: A form of self-esteem that reflects how good you feel about yourself in general or on average.

## Suggested Reading

Baumeister, Campbell, Krueger, and Vohs, "Exploding the Self-Esteem Myth."

Leary, "Sociometer Theory and the Pursuit of Relational Value."

1. According to sociometer theory, what does self-esteem do?

2. Although low self-esteem is associated with a number of psychological difficulties, there is virtually no evidence that low self-esteem causes these problems. If low self-esteem doesn't cause psychological and social problems, then why is low self-esteem related to them?

# Why Do We Have Emotions?

## Lecture 6

O ur lives are filled with emotions, and they play a very important role in the quality of our lives. In fact, the quality of each day depends on the kinds of emotions that you experience. Furthermore, because we like certain feelings more than others, much of our behavior is aimed toward seeking certain emotions and avoiding others. In this lecture, you'll learn what emotions are, why we have them, and what they do. Emotions aren't just about feelings; they also involve motives and bodily changes that prepare us to react to the important things that happen around us.

**Functions of Emotions**

- Virtually all emotions are fundamentally about physical safety and well-being or social safety and well-being. Emotions almost always arise in response to things that happen—or might happen—in our physical environment or our social environment.

- This doesn't mean that every time we experience an emotion, there's really a threat or benefit to our physical or social well-being. We create many emotions in our own minds even when nothing is happening. Our capacity to experience emotions evolved to help us deal with events that have implications for our physical and social well-being.

- Most people think of emotions in terms of the feelings that they experience, but scientists who study emotion view emotions as an interconnected system of thoughts, feelings, motives, and bodily reactions that work together to do three basic things.

- First, emotions notify us about important events—both good and bad. Emotions arise to focus our attention on some potentially important situation or event. Sometimes these events are risks, threats, costs—things that might compromise our well-being—but sometimes they're positive, such as opportunities, advantages, or benefits that we need to be aware of.

- We need to be aware of both the good and bad things that happen to us. Particularly in the case of bad things, emotions force us to focus on the event until we take action—if we can—and continue to make us feel bad until we do something. If we didn't have emotions, we might overlook or dismiss important things.

- The second thing that emotions do is motivate people to behave in ways that deal with the event. Every emotion is associated with a specific motivation or urge—an impulse to respond in a particular way, which is called an **action tendency**. However, we don't always act on this urge; sometimes, we force ourselves not to respond the way the action tendency is pushing us—but the urge is still there, and we can usually feel it.

- The third thing that emotions do is produce changes in the body, many of which are designed to prepare us to respond to whatever caused the emotion. For example, when people are afraid, their heart rate, respiration, and blood pressure increase; muscles tense up; and blood is shunted from the digestive system to the muscles. These changes prepare the body to respond to the fearful stimulus either by running away or, if it's an attacking person or animal, by fighting it.

- In addition to bodily changes that help us deal directly with the emotion-producing situation, some emotions are associated with bodily changes that convey our emotional state to other people. Often, our bodies automatically send signals to other people about what we're feeling, and then those signals lead other people to respond to us in particular ways.

**The Origin of Emotions**
- There's a lot of controversy among psychological scientists who study emotion about how many different emotions there are. In fact, some researchers think that it's not even a reasonable question

to ask how many emotions there are because there are almost an infinite number of shades and combinations of emotion that are defined by differences in their positive or negative valence, intensity, and other characteristics.

- A more interesting question regards what determines the emotion we feel at any particular time. Many people assume that they feel whatever emotion is elicited by the situation. However, there are instances in which three people experience the same event, but each of them reacts in a completely different way.

- In addition, sometimes you may feel different emotions at different times in response to exactly the same situation. Therefore, the objective event isn't what causes us to feel one emotion rather than another. Instead, our emotions are determined by our interpretations of events rather than the events themselves.

- **Cognitive appraisal theory** says that each specific emotion is elicited by a particular kind of cognitive appraisal, which is the person's assessment of the impact of the event on his or her well-being and personal concerns. Appraisals of how things affect us—in good and bad ways—can happen very quickly and sometimes without much conscious thought.

- In addition, these appraisals determine the specific emotion that we experience in any particular situation. Every emotion is caused by a specific kind of appraisal, and if you change the person's appraisal of the situation, you'll change his or her emotion.

- We sometimes think consciously about the effects that some situation or event might have on us and, as a result, experience some emotion. However, the appraisals that evoke emotions often occur automatically and unconsciously.

- The automatic and often nonconscious nature of cognitive appraisals is very beneficial. We can't go through life constantly thinking about whether everything that happens is good or bad;

instead, we seem to have a system that automatically scans our environment for things that have good or bad consequences for us.

- The fact that emotions are caused by cognitive appraisals has an important implication: People's appraisals are not always correct. For example, an event may appear potentially dangerous when it's actually not, but if you appraise it as harmful, you'll feel anxious or afraid—for absolutely no reason.

- There are many instances in which people experience emotions, even very strong emotions, when their feelings have no basis in reality—but they appraised a situation in such a way that caused a particular emotion.

- The problem is that it's difficult for any of us to know whether our appraisals are accurate. Of course, we each think that our view of the world is reasonably accurate, but it's often not, and we sometimes don't know for certain. Even when our appraisal of a situation or event is incorrect, we'll often experience the emotion that goes along with the appraisal.

- The things that cause other animals to respond emotionally are always real objects and events in their immediate environment. Just like human beings, other animals sometimes react to things that don't really matter, but they still only react emotionally to real events.

- Human beings are different. Sometimes the things that cause our emotions are tangible events in our immediate environment, but unlike other animals, we often induce emotions in ourselves just by thinking about things that are not actually real at the moment.

- These self-generated emotions are particularly interesting because, in most circumstances, they aren't very useful. Emotions don't do us much good if there's nothing we can do to take action at the time.

- The capacity for emotions evolved to notify us about threats and opportunities in our environment, to motivate appropriate actions, and to prepare the body to respond. But these emotional systems evolved before our prehistoric ancestors had the ability to self-reflect—to think consciously about themselves—as we can now.

- Throughout most of evolution, our ancestors were like other animals, responding to the threats and opportunities that they directly encountered. Because they lacked self-awareness, they couldn't conjure up images of themselves in the future and become upset about those imaginings. However, now we can imagine the future in our own mind, and those thoughts alone can create emotions.

- This suggests that we should be aware of the degree to which we unnecessarily inflict undesired emotions on ourselves just by thinking and imagining. Although having these emotions is perfectly normal, sometimes you can catch yourself and not allow yourself to get carried away with your imaginings.

## Shame and Schadenfreude

- There are a few emotions that are less easy to understand than fear, for example, and shame is one of these emotions. In everyday language, people often use shame and guilt as if they refer to the same emotion, but emotion research suggests that shame and guilt are two different experiences.

- Shame and guilt look superficially similar because they both start with some sort of a bad behavior—a misdeed that breaks moral rules or hurts somebody. However, once a person knows that that he or she has behaved badly, whether the person experiences guilt or shame depends on precisely how the person thinks about the bad behavior.

- Guilt is caused by a cognitive appraisal that focuses on the negative behavior itself, so when people recognize that they have done something bad, they feel guilty. However, when people go beyond the recognition that they performed a bad behavior to the conclusion that they are a bad person, they feel ashamed.

- Shame is a stronger, darker, and more powerful emotion than guilt. Shame feels worse, in part, because the kinds of misbehaviors that lead people to conclude that they are a bad person are often worse than the kinds of misbehaviors that are just bad behaviors. Beyond that, however, shame may be more intense than guilt because it includes self-recrimination.

- The action tendencies of guilt and shame are also different. When people feel guilty, their primary motive seems to be to fix the problem they have caused and make it up to anyone they've hurt. On the other hand, people who are experiencing shame become very self-focused; they tend to withdraw socially and focus mostly on how bad they are feeling about themselves.

© Digital Vision/Thinkstock.

**People who feel ashamed may become angry at themselves, but fixing the problem is not their primary concern.**

- There's a common belief that because shame is such a negative emotion, just the prospect of being ashamed helps to keep people's behavior in line. If that were true, then shame might have a preventative function in deterring bad behavior, but that does not appear to be the case.

- When researchers have compared people who are more likely to feel guilty to those who are more likely to feel ashamed, they find that people who experience guilt are likely to behave in moral and prosocial ways. However, the more that people tend to feel shame, the more likely they are to misbehave.

- While we can trace a possible function for feelings of guilt, researchers have had a difficult time seeing that shame does anything useful—either for the individual who feels ashamed or the people that they've hurt.

- Another emotion that is not well understood is **Schadenfreude**, which is the pleasure that people experience over the misfortunes of another person. Normally, we feel bad, or at least indifferent, when bad things happen to other people, but sometimes we actually experience a bit of pleasure.

- There are a couple of puzzling things about Schadenfreude. Is Schadenfreude genuinely a distinct emotion, or is it just pleasure— specifically, pleasure that is caused by another person's misfortune? What is its action tendency, or what does Schadenfreude motivate people to do? We don't have the answers to these questions.

## Important Terms

**action tendency**: An impulse to respond in a particular way as a result of a specific emotion.

**cognitive appraisal theory**: A theory that claims that each specific emotion is elicited by a particular kind of cognitive appraisal, which is the person's assessment of the impact of the event on his or her well-being and personal concerns.

**Schadenfreude**: The pleasure that people experience over the misfortunes of another person.

## Suggested Reading

D'Amato, "Mystery of Disgust."

Frank, *Passions Within Reason*.

## Questions to Consider

1. What three basic things do emotions do in response to threats and opportunities that people experience?

2. What are the appraisals and action tendencies for each of the following emotions: fear, anger, disgust, guilt, and awe?

# What Makes People Happy?
## Lecture 7

In the previous lecture, you learned about the nature of emotions in general. Next, you're going to analyze a few specific emotions in greater detail—starting in this lecture with happiness, which is what most people say they want most in life. You will learn that life situations and bad experiences contribute to people's desperation and unhappiness, but not nearly as much as most people assume. People's day-to-day happiness and well-being depend far more on how they approach life than on what life brings. This understanding will hopefully open the door to greater happiness and life satisfaction for you.

**Sources of Happiness**

- People have been trying to figure out the source of happiness for thousands of years, but only in the past couple of decades have psychologists and other behavioral scientists started to study happiness scientifically. Scientific research suggests that most of the things that people believe will make them happy actually won't—at least not in the long run.

- Social psychologist Sonja Lyubomirsky is one of the world's authorities on happiness, and her research shows that the causes of happiness can be classified into three major categories: life circumstances, genetics, and behavior.

- Furthermore, her research shows that only about 10 percent of people's happiness is due to their life circumstances—such as their jobs, relationships, financial situation, family situation, and health. However, that's what most of us focus on and try to change to make us happier. This data implies that your life circumstances might make you happy, but perhaps they don't make you as happy as you think they do—or for as long as you might imagine.

- Many people think that they will be happier if they had more money. Research shows that it's certainly difficult to be truly happy if you live in poverty; if you're always hungry, cold, living in unsafe surroundings, or always owe somebody money, happiness can be elusive.

- As a result, below a certain income level, poor people are less happy and less satisfied with their lives than most people. However, above the poverty level, things are complicated. Researchers at Princeton University found that up until an income of somewhere between $60,000 and $75,000, more money is associated with feeling a bit more happy.

- The reason that money increases happiness up to a point seems to be that having a certain amount of money helps to fix certain problems in life that make people stressed out and unhappy. Furthermore, after people have somewhere between $60,000 and $75,000, there's no relationship between income and happiness.

- Many people have trouble reconciling this finding with the fact that they know that they feel happy, for example, when they get a raise at work—even a small raise—but this is a very fleeting feeling. Many people think that money will bring them a lot of happiness for a long time, but it actually brings them only a little happiness for a short time.

- Another thing that many people think would make them happier is if they were more physically attractive, but studies show that happier people are not any more physically attractive than unhappy people are.

- Many people think that there is a relationship between physical appearance and happiness, however, so they put a lot of effort into looking good, and some people even turn to cosmetic surgery to look better. For a short time after their surgery, they're often very pleased with the results, but after a few months, they're not any happier than they were beforehand.

- The problem is that people tend to adjust to pleasurable changes in their circumstances. Psychologists call this pattern **hedonic adaptation**: We adapt emotionally to improvements in our life situation, so something that initially brings happiness and pleasure usually wears off over time.

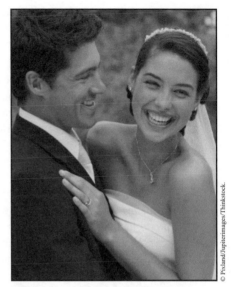

- For example, most people view marriage as a happy event, and marriage does make people happier for awhile, but then people

**Most people view marriage as a happy event, but once people adapt to being married, their happiness declines.**

adapt to being married and their happiness slowly returns to where they were before they got married. For some couples, it even turns negative after awhile.

## Affective Forecasting

- Even though we've all experienced hedonic adaptation many times in our lives, for some reason, we don't expect it to happen. When we think about future events, we expect both good and bad feelings to last longer than they really do. People are not good at **affective forecasting**—in predicting how events will influence their emotions in the long run.

- Social psychologists have conducted many studies of affective forecasting, and this research consistently shows that people almost always overestimate how good or how bad they will feel when things happen—as well as how long their good or bad feelings will last.

- One reason that we are so bad at forecasting how happy or upset events will make us feel is **focalism**, which describes the notion that when people think about how they will feel about some event in the future, they focus too much on the event itself and ignore all of the other things that will be going on that will influence their emotions.

- In addition, a second reason that people are bad at affective forecasting is that they underestimate how well they will cope with problems that arise. People have the ability to make the best out of pretty bad situations, but when forecasting their emotions, people tend to neglect the role that their coping resources will play in reducing their negative emotions.

- Unfortunately, our poor ability to predict how happy something will make us feel can lead to some pretty bad decisions. Almost every decision that we make, big or small, is based partly on our guesses about what will ultimately make us happy. If we often misjudge the long-term impact of events on our happiness, then we are sometimes going to make bad decisions, and upon looking back, we often feel disappointed that our choice didn't make us as happy as we had expected.

## Genes and Happiness

- Research suggests that only about 10 percent of people's happiness is due to their life circumstances and that about 50 percent of it is due to people's genetic make-up, which you can't do much about. Genes play an important role in people's personalities, including how they tend to respond to what happens to them.

- Our genes determine the structure and activity of our brains: Some people's brains are structured in ways that promote positive emotions, and some people have brains that respond more easily to negative emotions. Many studies have conclusively shown that about 50 percent of the variability that we see in the degree to which people experience positive and negative emotions is due to genetic factors.

- For example, research shows that identical twins are more similar in their level of happiness—or unhappiness—than siblings who are not twins, even if the twins have been separated at birth and raised by different families. Their identical genes create identical brains that make them similar in how happy—or unhappy—they are. They won't be identical in happiness, however, because genetic influences account for only 50 percent of happiness.

- The best way to think about genetic influences is to think of yourself as having some typical baseline of happiness. Good events will temporarily increase your happiness, and bad events will make you unhappy. However, after those events have passed and nothing particularly good or bad is going on in your life, you will return again to your own typical baseline—almost as if it's a set point.

- After we account for the 50 percent of happiness that's due to genetic factors and the 10 percent that's due to life circumstances, the remaining 40 percent is due to intentional behavior—what we do and how we think. People who are happier do things differently than people who are less happy. Research suggests that if we all do things the way that happy people do, we'll be happier, too.

## Subjective Well-Being

- When people imagine a really happy person, they often think of someone smiling or laughing who is experiencing a surge of pleasure because something good has happened to them. However, what most people want more than occasional episodes of happiness is an overriding sense of contentment and pleasure—a sense of well-being that goes deeper than happiness. This notion of **subjective well-being** is different from momentary happiness.

- People who generally live with a sense of high subjective well-being differ from people who report lower subjective well-being in the degree to which their lives are characterized by **eudaemonia**, which can be defined as living one's life in a way that focuses on things that are intrinsically important for human well-being.

- Some goals are more intrinsically important to your well-being, meaning that they are pursued for their own sake rather than to get something else. Spending more time with your children or friends can be an intrinsic goal because you probably truly want to spend more time with them—not so that you can obtain some other goal.

- On the other hand, making money is not an intrinsic goal. You don't want to make money just to have piles of money; you want money because it will allow you to obtain or do other things. Money isn't intrinsically rewarding in the same way that you may find it intrinsically rewarding to spend time with people you love, for example.

- Eudaemonia, which involves living in a way that focuses on things that are intrinsically important, seems to be related to higher subjective well-being, which means that people are most likely to experience subjective well-being when they are seeking things that are intrinsically important.

- Studies have shown that attaining intrinsic goals improves subjective well-being whereas attaining extrinsic goals is usually irrelevant to subjective well-being. This pattern of findings may explain why certain behaviors are associated with greater happiness and subjective well-being while other behaviors are not.

- Of course, none of us can focus only on intrinsic goals that are inherently important to us; all of us must do many things for extrinsic reasons, and we often don't have much control over many of those extrinsically motivated activities. Nevertheless, happier people are able to add intrinsically satisfying goals to their lives—such as hobbies, community service, and spending time with loved ones—that will lead them to have a greater well-being.

- Research shows that happier people are committed to certain long-term, maybe even lifetime, goals that they regularly pursue. Perhaps most importantly, research consistently shows that happier people put more time and effort into their relationships with other people.

- However, just because happy people engage in intrinsically important activities doesn't necessarily mean that they are happy because they do these things. Maybe being happy makes people behave in these ways. Being happy does lead to better behavior, but behaving in these ways also leads people to feel more happy. The direction of causality goes in both ways.

## Important Terms

**affective forecasting**: The act of predicting how events will influence one's emotions in the long run.

**eudaemonia**: The act of living one's life in a way that focuses on things that are intrinsically important for human well-being.

**focalism**: The notion that when people think about how they will feel about some event in the future, they focus too much on the event itself and ignore all of the other things that will be going on that will influence their emotions.

**hedonic adaptation**: The tendency for people adjust to pleasurable changes in their circumstances so that something that initially brings happiness and pleasure usually wears off over time.

**subjective well-being**: An overriding sense of contentment and pleasure; a sense of well-being that goes deeper than happiness.

## Suggested Reading

Lyubomirsky, *The How of Happiness*.

Pawelski, "The Many Faces of Happiness."

1. Research suggests that 40 percent of people's happiness is under their control. What contributes to the other 60 percent?

2. Explain the role that hedonic adaptation plays in people's happiness.

# Why Are So Many People So Stressed Out?
## Lecture 8

Stress takes a major toll on both the psychological and physical well-being of many people. People who are under stress are often moody and hostile, and chronic stress leads some people to become depressed. Stress interferes with people's ability to perform well at work and school, and it takes a tremendous toll on people's health. Stress is such a serious and common problem that it's not an understatement to suggest that there is a stress epidemic. In this lecture, you'll discover the common causes of stress and the different ways in which people with different personalities deal with stress.

**The Origin of Stress**
- To understand the causes of stress, we need to make a distinction between acute stress and chronic stress. **Acute stress** occurs when people experience an immediate threat to their well-being. It is a normal part of life for all animals, including human beings.

- When you receive a piece of bad news or lose your wallet, the stress response kicks in as nature's way of helping you respond to the event. Once the event is over, your body returns to normal and acute stress goes away, with little or no lingering effects.

- When people talk about being under stress, they're usually talking about **chronic stress**—stress that's almost always there. Even when a person is doing something else, chronic stress is in the background ready to rise up at any time. Most animals don't appear to experience chronic stress.

- The only animals that seem to show signs of chronic stress are some that live around human beings. Animals that are kept in cages or abused by people show signs of chronic stress, but when left alone, far away from people, animals don't appear to experience chronic stress the way that people do.

- The first reason that people are far more chronically stressed out than other animals is that we live in an environment that is drastically different from the environment in which our brains evolved. Wild animals, though, live in essentially the same sorts of environments in which they have been living for millions of years, so their brains are adapted to responding to the challenging and stressful features of those environments.

- Many—in fact, maybe most—of the things that create chronic stress in our everyday lives are the recent developments of civilization and culture, including traffic jams, computer crashes, constant noise, air travel, and stock market declines. In some ways, it's amazing that people manage in their new environment as well as they do. Of course, many of the advances and innovations that stress us out have also improved our lives immensely.

- The second reason that many people are stressed out involves the fact that we live with a lot of uncertainty regarding whether life is going well. Animals in the wild live in an **immediate-return environment**, in which an animal can see the consequences of its behavior on an ongoing basis. It gets immediate feedback regarding whether it is accomplishing essential life tasks.

- About 10,000 years ago—at the start of the agricultural revolution— people began to settle into permanent communities, acquire land and possessions, and grow their own food. When people started relying on farming, they suddenly found themselves in a **delayed-return environment**, in which people invest a lot of time and effort each day into tasks that don't have any immediate rewards, without knowing whether their efforts will pay off in the future.

- Much of the stress of modern life comes from the fact that we live in a profoundly delayed-return environment. If you have a job or are going to school, not much of what you do each day provides for your needs on that day; instead, you probably spend much of your time each day thinking about, planning for, working toward, and worrying about your future goals.

- In addition, as you put all of your time and effort into work or school on a particular day, you have no assurance that your hard work will necessarily pay off later. As a result, people experience stress over whether they will get a job after college or will achieve other long-term goals. The uncertainty about the future is stressful.

- A third reason that people are so stressed out—and other animals aren't—is because there's often nothing we can do to solve the problems that worry us. In an immediate-return environment, most stressors exist in the moment, so people can usually do something immediately that might deal with the acute stressor. Their actions may not be effective in dealing with the problem, and they might not survive, but at least they can usually take action. However, when the things that create stress lie in the future, as they often do for us, the threat is in our mind rather than immediately present.

A deer may experience acute stress when it is startled by a loud noise, but it doesn't experience chronic stress as humans do.

## Common Sources of Chronic Stress

- When researchers examine the kinds of things that produce chronic stress—the major categories of stressful events and situations—they come up with five sources of stress. These major categories of stressors are exceptionally common, which also helps to explain why so many people are so stressed out, and they are virtually unavoidable in modern life.

- The most common chronic source of stress for Americans is money. Even in developed countries—such as the United States, where the standard of living is high on average—many people don't have enough money to pay the bills. Furthermore, even people who have enough money for the basics of life live with the chronic stress of knowing that they don't have enough for the extra expenses that will arise.

- Personal relationships also add to people's stress. Of course, relationships—whether with friends, partners, or family members—are often a great source of pleasure and support, but relationships are also cauldrons of stress.

- People also experience a lot of stress because of work and school. Studies show that less than 50 percent of employees are happy with their jobs, and many people live with the constant threat of losing their job. Likewise, academic pressures put students under a lot of chronic stress.

- Health problems are a fourth major source of stress. Being ill or injured, learning that you have a serious medical condition, or discovering that you must undergo medical procedures are major causes of stress for everybody at one time or another in their lives.

- In addition to these four categories, we are stressed out by what might seem to be relatively trivial situations and events: the daily hassles and irritants that we experience on an ongoing basis. Most of these experiences are unavoidable, and they add to the stress that people experience.

### Type A Personality and Neuroticism
- Stress is a part of life, but people differ in how well they cope with the stresses in their lives. Some people seem to come unglued at every turn and have lots of stress-induced problems; other people seem to roll with the punches a little better.

- In thinking about how people's personalities relate to their ability to handle stress, it's useful to consider how stressful events unfold. When people are exposed to a stressful situation or event, they evaluate the situation and then try to cope with the situation in some way.

- There are four points in this stress sequence where one person might experience more or less stress than another person: People might experience a lot of stress because they are exposed to more stressful events, judge events as more threatening, don't think that they can cope well with the stressful situation, or try to cope with it in ways that aren't very effective.

- People who have a type A personality experience more stress—and are more likely to have health problems that are due to stress, such as heart disease—than people who are low in type A. Type A people genuinely experience more stressful events because they live their lives in ways that create a high level of stress.

- Type A people have been described as being engaged in an incessant struggle to do more and more in less and less time; people who have a type A personality create lives for themselves in which they have too much to do. As a result, they experience chronic stress from trying to squeeze too many things into too little time.

- In addition, a central aspect of being type A is having a sense of time urgency—the sense of never having enough time to get everything done—which can be stressful for anyone. However, the reason that people who are high in type A don't have enough time is because they try to do too much. They experience a lot of frustration and stress when things don't happen as quickly as they would like, particularly when they feel that they are being slowed down. Traffic jams and long checkout lines set off a strong stress reaction for type A people.

- Another personality characteristic that is associated with high stress is neuroticism, which involves the degree to which people experience negative emotions—such as anger, anxiety, sadness, and stress. They experience greater stress when severely negative events happen, but they also are more upset by minor daily hassles.

- One reason that people who are high in neuroticism experience greater stress is that they are more likely to interpret ordinary situations as threatening and to view minor frustrations as hopelessly difficult. They don't necessarily experience more negative events, but they find ordinary problems and hassles more stressful.

- The amount of stress that people experience depends heavily on how they interpret situations, and people high in neuroticism interpret situations more negatively.

## Self-Compassion
- A characteristic that's associated with lower stress is **self-compassion**, which involves the degree to which people treat themselves in a kind and caring way when bad things happen. When many people experience failure, rejection, embarrassment, or loss, they are really hard on themselves—particularly when the situation is their fault.

- However, some people are particularly forgiving and kind toward themselves when things go badly. They treat themselves with the same kind of caring and concern that they show their loved ones when bad things happen. Recent research shows that people who are self-compassionate experience less stress—as well as less negative emotions of all kinds—than people who are not self-compassionate.

- Whether they're dealing with major life stressors or minor stressors and hassles, people who are self-compassionate deal much better with stressful events for two reasons: They don't heap unnecessary self-criticism on themselves when things go badly, and they actually go out of their way to be nice to themselves when stressful events occur.

- Stress is a major problem for many people—one that undermines the quality of their lives and can lead to a variety of health problems as well. Of course, a certain amount of stress is unavoidable, but we also create a lot of the stress that we experience. In either case, knowing how to cope with life in ways that minimize stress is an important life skill.

## Important Terms

**acute stress**: The type of stress that occurs when people experience an immediate threat to their well-being.

**chronic stress**: The type of stress that almost always exists.

**delayed-return environment**: An environment in which people invest a great deal of time and effort each day into tasks that don't have any immediate rewards, without knowing whether their efforts will pay off in the future.

**immediate-return environment**: An environment in which people can see the consequences of their behavior on an ongoing basis and receive immediate feedback regarding whether they are accomplishing essential life tasks.

**self-compassion**: The degree to which people treat themselves in a kind and caring way when bad things happen.

## Suggested Reading

Neff, *Self-Compassion*.

Sapolsky, *Why Zebras Don't Get Ulcers*.

1. Why do people live under so much more chronic stress than animals living in the wild?

2. Why do people who score high in neuroticism and type A experience greater stress than people who score low on these personality characteristics?

# Why Do Hurt Feelings Hurt?
## Lecture 9

P eople's social relationships are critically important to their well-being, and they were undoubtedly even more important in the prehistoric past. Hurt feelings let people know when their connections with other people might be damaged. The common element to all instances of hurt feelings—the cognitive appraisal that leads to hurt feelings—involves perceiving that we have less relational value to another person or group than we would like to have. In this lecture, you will learn the kinds of events that hurt people's feelings and why hurt feelings hurt like they do.

### Emotional Research

- Researchers have been interested in emotions since the earliest days of psychological science. Although there has been lots of research on a wide array of emotions—such as fear, sadness, anger, jealousy, disgust, guilt, and embarrassment—until the mid-1990s, there was almost no mention of hurt feelings in the research literature on emotions. Everybody has their feelings hurt at some point, so it's not an unusual experience, but researchers didn't pay much attention to it until the more recent past.

- Virtually all of the hurtful situations that people describe fall into one of six broad categories. The largest category involves explicit cases of rejection—instances in which other people make it absolutely clear that they don't want to have anything to do with a person. These situations include ending a close relationship and being fired.

- The second largest category of hurtful situations involves circumstances in which people aren't explicitly rejected, but they feel that others are avoiding or ignoring them. For example, people feel hurt when another person doesn't return their phone calls or when other people don't seem interested in hanging out with them.

- A third broad category of hurtful events involves being criticized. People can certainly criticize others without actually rejecting them, but certain criticisms still hurt people's feelings.

- The fourth category involves hurtful episodes in which someone betrays another. Many of these include classic betrayals by romantic partners, but other kinds of betrayals include a family member divulging one's personal secrets or a friend starting to date someone that a person likes.

- In the fifth category are instances where people are hurt by malicious teasing. Of course, good-natured teasing can signify closeness and liking, but mean teasing can be really hurtful.

- Finally, a sixth category of hurtful events involves feeling unappreciated or taken for granted. These aren't instances where there is actually rejection, but these types of events still hurt people's feelings.

**Cognitive Appraisal**
- Each emotion is characterized by a specific cognitive appraisal. For example, an appraisal of possible harm leads to fear, and an appraisal that one has made a bad impression on other people leads to embarrassment. We might assume that people's feelings are hurt when they are rejected, but although a couple of the categories of hurtful events clearly involve rejection, some of them don't. Being criticized, teased, or unappreciated doesn't necessarily involve being rejected.

- Hurt feelings are caused by the appraisal that a person's **relational value** to another person is lower than he or she wants it to be, at least at the moment when the pain is felt. Hurt feelings are caused by low perceived relational value.

- Each of us realizes that other people value their relationships with us to varying degrees. There are people who value their relationships with you a great deal; you can tell that they consider their relationship with you to be very important. You also know other people who value their relationships with you somewhat less. Then, there are some people who value their relationship with you very little—if at all.

- We usually don't care that certain people value their relationships with us to different degrees or that certain people that we have to deal with really don't care about their relationship with us at all. We couldn't maintain important relationships with everybody anyway, so it's OK that not everybody values their relationship with us.

- However, when we perceive from another person's behavior that he or she values our relationship less than we desire—that our relational value in the person's eyes is lower than we want it to be—that's when our feelings get hurt. You experience hurt feelings when you perceive that your relational value to some person, or group of people, is lower than you would like it to be.

- Outright rejection is a pretty clear case of having low relational value, so it's no surprise that being explicitly rejected hurts people's feelings. Rejection wouldn't necessarily hurt us, though, if we didn't care whether the other person valued his or her relationship with us. However, when we want others to value their relationship with us, then rejection hurts us because it's obvious that they don't value their relationship with us as much as we'd like.

- Explicit rejection isn't necessary to hurt our feelings. For example, criticism doesn't necessarily involve rejection; in fact, it usually doesn't. However, criticism can convey low relational value because being criticized shows that the other person evaluates something about us negatively, and having undesirable characteristics presumably undermines the value of our relationship to the other person.

- Being criticized implies that another person has reasons not to value us as much as we might like them to. Sometimes just the fact that another person says something negative to us may make us think that they don't value our relationship very much—even if the criticism is accurate.

- Being betrayed obviously conveys that we have low relational value. People don't betray those whose relationships they fully value. Likewise, being maliciously teased conveys that the teaser doesn't value his or her relationship with us. People don't tease and torment people whose relationships they value.

## Physical Pain versus Hurt Feelings

- Pain is nature's way of getting our attention and telling us that something is happening that threatens our well-being. If we didn't feel pain, we'd constantly injure ourselves and not even know it.

- In addition, just knowing that certain things hurt keeps us from behaving in ways that might injure or kill us. The possibility of pain discourages us from engaging in dangerous behaviors. In fact, people who can't experience pain—those who are born with congenital analgesia, for example—have to work very hard not to injure or kill themselves accidentally.

- The feelings of hurt that come from having low relational value serve exactly the same function—to protect us. Throughout human evolutionary history, people couldn't afford to be indifferent to whether others accepted or rejected them because they couldn't survive if they lived on their own. Social rejection was a death sentence.

- Now, evolutionary processes are efficient. They don't build brand new bodily systems to do things if they don't need to, so there are many cases in which a system that evolved initially for one purpose was later co-opted to do something else.

- The biological systems that make us feel physical pain evolved to warn us about physical harm and to keep us from doing things that damaged our bodies. Then, probably millions of years later, evolution used some of the same neural circuitry that was originally involved in physical pain to also warn us about threats to our social connections.

- In the 1970s, researchers discovered that neurotransmitters in the brain that play a role in processing physical pain are also involved in reactions to social separation. For example, the neurotransmitters that are involved in pain are also involved when babies cry when they are separated from their mothers.

© George Doyle/Stockbyte/Thinkstock.

**When people talk about rejection, they usually describe it in terms that are similar to those that describe physical pain.**

- Medications, such as morphine, that reduce physical pain also decrease the distress cries of babies who are separated from their mothers. Researchers have found this effect not only in human babies, but also among the infants of many other species of mammals as well.

- In addition to the same neurotransmitters being involved in physical pain and social distress, certain areas of the brain are as well. When you are in pain, you may not realize that your experience consists of two distinct components: a sensory component of pain that provides information about the location in your body where the painful stimulation is coming from and an emotional, or affective, component to the experience of pain.

- When you're in pain, you feel psychologically distressed. Even though the physical sensation of pain is at a specific body location, you have an awful, desperate psychological feeling as

71

well. Researchers who have mapped the areas of the brain that are involved in pain have found that the physical component of pain and the emotional, or psychological, component of pain are mediated by different brain regions.

- In fact, people who have certain kinds of brain surgery for chronic pain report that they can still feel the pain in their body, but it doesn't bother them as much psychologically as it did before the surgery. The sensory component of pain is still there, but the affective component—the psychological distress—is gone.

- Conversely, damage to other parts of the brain disrupts people's ability to tell where they hurt—where the painful stimulation is coming from—but they still experience the psychological distress. For those people, the sensory component of pain is gone, but they experience the emotional, psychological component.

- The hurt feelings that people experience when they are not relationally valued appear to use the psychological, emotional component of the pain system. Neuroimaging studies, in which researchers scan people's brains, show that some of the same parts of the brain that are involved in the emotional component of physical pain are activated when people are rejected.

- The fact that the brain systems that underlie physical pain overlap with the systems that are involved in psychological hurt caused by low relational value raises the interesting possibility that people who are more sensitive to physical pain are also more sensitive to getting their feelings hurt. Research shows that this is the case.

- In addition, neuroimaging studies show that people don't find painful stimuli as painful when someone who cares about them is present—or even when they look at a picture of a loved one. Perhaps this is because feeling valued and accepted reduces activity in the pain regions of the brain so that painful medical procedures don't hurt as much.

- Furthermore, brain imaging studies have confirmed that because physical pain and hurt feelings use some of the same brain architecture, the same medications that reduce physical pain also lower hurt feelings.

- Although physical pain and social pain are not precisely the same, they do involve some common brain regions that make certain social experiences genuinely hurt. Additionally, physical and social pain both serve a similar purpose: warning us of events that pose a possible threat to our well-being and deterring us from doing things that will lead to harm.

## Important Term

**relational value**: The amount of value that is placed on a relationship between people.

## Suggested Reading

MacDonald and Leary, "Why Does Social Exclusion Hurt?"

Williams, "The Pain of Exclusion."

## Questions to Consider

1. What do all situations that hurt people's feelings have in common?

2. From a neurological standpoint, why are hurt feelings painful?

# Why Do We Make Mountains out of Molehills?
## Lecture 10

People have a normal and adaptive drive to watch out for their own interests and to try to get other people to conform to their wishes. In addition, everybody becomes frustrated, disappointed, and even angry when things don't go as planned. The problem occurs when the otherwise useful psychological system that protects people's self-interest by leading them to stand up for themselves sometimes reacts too strongly or under circumstances that are not appropriate. Because people who are in a state of overreaction aren't attuned to the things that normally monitor inappropriate behavior, their reactions can get out of control.

### Overreacting to Disrespect

- No animal can survive that doesn't have its own well-being as its top priority; every animal must fundamentally look after itself. Like all other animals, human beings respond strongly to events that threaten their well-being.

- People fight to defend themselves and their loved ones against physical attack, resist efforts to take their possessions or money, and become angry when their freedom or rights are violated. We can't let people harm and take advantage of us, so it's natural and reasonable to become upset when our well-being is at stake.

- However, people often react strongly to events that pose little or no tangible threat to them. People overreact to trivial frustrations, minor annoyances, and little inconveniences in ways that far exceed the response needed to deal with the situation.

- Sometimes these overreactions are not a big deal, but at other times, these overreactions are far more serious. Whether they are minor fits or lethal violence, these kinds of overreactions are puzzling because they almost always bring about more costs than rewards for the person who has overreacted.

- The capacity for emotional experience evolved to help animals deal with important threats and opportunities in their physical and social environments, but instances in which people display excessive emotional and behavioral reactions that go far beyond the implications of an event for their well-being raise questions about why people overreact. Overreacting takes energy, hurts other people's feelings, damages relationships, and can even result in legal problems—but people overreact anyway.

- It's certainly true that some people are more likely to overreact than other people, but just about everyone overreacts from time to time. One common cause of angry overreactions is disrespect. Research shows that people often overreact when they are treated disrespectfully—even when nothing tangible is at stake. Just indications of disrespect can set people off.

- On the surface, reacting to disrespect when it really doesn't matter may seem irrational, but researchers suggest that there are sometimes good reasons to stand up to implied disrespect even when it doesn't matter at the moment—including the fact that reacting strongly puts people on notice that the person should not be trifled with.

- People may respond to cases of inconsequential disrespect or unfairness to deter more serious infractions later, and the stronger the person responds, the more effective it will be in showing others that the person will not be taken advantage of. Evolutionary psychologists suggest that this reaction may be built into human nature. Many other mammals show this kind of hair-trigger reaction to other animals who aren't actually threatening their well-being at the moment.

- Many species, including wolves and chimpanzees, will attack and kill an unfamiliar member of their species that merely wanders into their territory. From an animal's standpoint, there are benefits of such extreme reactions to an objectively trivial behavior. In nature, it's better to address possible problems in the moment than wait until the intruder actually does something harmful.

- In fact, a tendency to respond strongly in such situations was probably favored by natural selection. It's possible that human beings carry this evolved tendency to address possible problems in the moment, which makes us overreact to rather minor signs that other people are not treating us as we would like. Overreactions to trivial provocations appear to be particularly common in situations in which such reactions are needed to prevent oneself from being mistreated.

- Many instances of overreactions involve disrespect, but they don't account for the full range of situations to which people overreact. More importantly, they don't explain the extremity of people's reactions. It's not just that people stand up for themselves, it's that they sometimes lose control in ways that far exceed what's needed to solve the problem and that are often ineffective or counterproductive.

- One intriguing piece of the puzzle is that when people are overreacting, they often seem to be in an altered state of consciousness. They have lost touch with the situation that they're in, and they don't seem to have control over their own behavior. In fact, sometimes people later say that they weren't aware of how out of control they really were until the episode was over.

- Furthermore, they often realize that other people are upset, that they've made a fool out of themselves, and that they did things that damaged their relationships with other people. Sometimes they even did things to damage their own possessions.

- What seems to happen is that the person becomes narrowly focused on what he or she wants to happen, and the person becomes so fixated on having this one desire fulfilled that other relevant considerations—such as social norms, moral standards, other people's feelings, or long-term consequences of their reaction—are ignored.

## The Origin of Overreaction

- Presumably, people have overreacted throughout history, but some cultural observers suggest that the types of overreactions that we see in American society today differ in certain respects from those of earlier generations.

- Not too long ago, people who were unable to control their anger were seen as weak and as having a character flaw of some kind. People seemed to regard anger as dangerous and disruptive and tried to control their reactions.

- There were times when anger was viewed as justified and even necessary, but being able to control one's anger and not overreact was seen as a virtue. In fact, the cultural heroes were often people who showed self-control even in the face of great provocation. People used to view angry overreactions as a reluctant last resort.

- In modern times, however, many people seem to feel entitled to react strongly to virtually anything that they don't like. In fact, to not vent your anger strongly is sometimes considered a sign of being inauthentic. Therefore, we see a lot of indignation and anger over things that would not have provoked open anger a generation or two ago, and very little of the anger that people express is about anything fundamentally important.

- Almost everyone overreacts to minor events from time to time, but some people show a consistent pattern of responding to frustrations, snubs, and signs of disrespect with explosive anger. Whereas most people may get angry only occasionally, people who are prone to anger report getting angry several days a week, and some people say they get angry virtually every day. People who become angry that often have a general tendency to overreact.

- We can gain some insight into why people overreact in general by examining the patterns of thought that are displayed by people with anger problems because the thoughts that make some people chronically angry are the same kinds of thoughts that all of us have when we overreact to minor events.

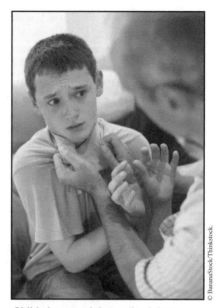

© BananaStock/Thinkstock.

- People with chronic anger problems tend to grossly exaggerate the seriousness of the things that happen to them—and, as a matter of fact, so do the rest of us at those times that we overreact. When people

**Child abuse and domestic violence often involve overreactions to extremely trivial events.**

overreact, they are often engaging in a **catastrophizing** thinking process, in which they have an exaggerated view of the likelihood that something bad is going to happen or an exaggerated belief about how bad the bad thing is.

- Catastrophizing underlies many overreactions because when people exaggerate the seriousness of a problem in their own mind, they naturally react more strongly than the situation objectively requires.

- Another type of thought that instigates angry overreactions is condemnation. When bad things happen, people often go beyond the fact that an undesired event occurred to a condemnation of the person who caused the undesired event.

- Condemnation and blame make us react more strongly to the undesired event than we otherwise would. A lot of research shows that condemnation fuels anger, hatred, and aggression.

- Generally, condemnation is misplaced. Most of the people who do things to us that we don't like are not evil, worthless people who are trying to hurt us. They might be careless, forgetful, lazy, or inconsiderate, but they're usually not awful people. However, when things don't go as we would like, we start to see people in those ways, which makes us react more strongly to minor events than we should.

## Expressing Strong Emotions

- Some people argue that it's good to express strong emotions—and to express them strongly—because it's an effective, and even healthy, way to reduce anger and aggressive feelings.

- The idea that it is cathartic to release one's emotions has a long history, going back at least to ancient Greece. It found its way into psychology through Sigmund Freud, who thought that **catharsis**, purging one's emotions, is helpful because people's emotions exist in a closed hydraulic system like a boiler or pressure cooker. Freud believed that when emotional pressure builds up in this system, people experience psychological problems, so they need to relieve the pressure from time to time to remain psychologically healthy.

- Catharsis continues to be endorsed today in a lot of pop psychology in which people are urged to express their anger—if not directly toward the person who upset them, at least toward inanimate objects. However, years of research have generally failed to find support for the catharsis hypothesis. In fact, if the goal is to reduce anger and aggression, doing nothing is better than venting one's anger. Instead of releasing anger, behaving aggressively activates more aggressive thoughts, emotions, and behaviors.

- Researchers who have studied episodes of anger find that at least half the time, situations in which people become angry with someone end badly. Normally, asserting one's views sternly will achieve the desired effect as much as boiling anger does, without the additional fallout and downstream consequences.

- It certainly feels natural to strike out when you are angry, and if you can't lash out at the person who angered you, it may seem useful to strike out at other things. However, contrary to what you might expect, striking out doesn't release your anger.

- Striking out is not designed to make us feel better or reduce our anger. The reason that we have the urge to strike out when we're angry is to coerce other people to do what we want them do to—to stop them from behaving in ways that frustrate our goals.

## Important Terms

**catastrophizing:** A thinking process in which a person has an exaggerated view of the likelihood that something bad is going to happen or an exaggerated belief about how bad the bad thing is.

**catharsis**: The act of purging one's emotions.

## Suggested Reading

Mauss, "Control Your Anger."

Tavris, *Anger*.

## Questions to Consider

1. Why may it sometimes be important for people living in certain situations to react strongly to minor signs of disrespect even when nothing important is at stake?

2. When people overreact strongly to minor frustrations and problems, the factors that normally control their behavior no longer seem to do so. Why?

# Why Is Self-Control So Hard?
## Lecture 11

E ach time we want to make ourselves do something that we don't want to do or try to resist the temptation to do something that we shouldn't do, we are up against many obstacles that interfere with successful self-control. Often, we fail. We are not designed to be paragons of self-control, so we just have to accept the fact that we have to work extra hard when we find ourselves pulled in different directions by competing desires. At present, the physiological processes that underlie self-control—and the depletion of self-control—remain a mystery.

**Self-Control versus Temptation**

- Problems with self-control almost always involve a conflict between two competing goals or motives—what psychologists call a **dual-motive conflict**. In most instances in which people don't control their behavior successfully, they are in a dual-motive conflict, being drawn in different directions by competing desires.

- When this happens, the goals that are in conflict often differ in how abstract and distant versus concrete and immediate they are. Concrete and immediate goals are more compelling and powerful than abstract and distant goals. In the moment that the person faces a dual–motive conflict, abstract, distant goals usually don't feel as strong—even though they are often more important.

- To make matters worse, distant goals don't seem worth as much as immediate goals; in other words, the consequences of a person's actions seem less important the further the consequences are in the future. Researchers call this effect **temporal discounting**: People discount outcomes that are further away in time.

- Important goals often involve things that will happen in the future. For example, losing weight might take months or even years. The same applies with negative outcomes: Punishments don't seem as bad when they are in the distant future as when they are going to happen soon. Therefore, distant punishments don't deter us as much from doing bad things as immediate punishments do.

- Two things are working against us when we face dual-motive conflicts: Abstract rewards are not as compelling as concrete rewards, and consequences that we will receive in the future seem worth less to us than immediate consequences. Unfortunately, the goal that we are often working for—to lose weight or to be healthy, for example—is both more abstract and more distant than the goal to enjoy tempting behaviors in the moment.

- Successful self-control often involves finding a way to promote our abstract and distant goals even in the face of immediate and concrete competing goals. People must do extra work in their own mind to make the important, abstract, distant goal more immediate and specific so that it can compete successfully with the specific and immediate temptation.

- One recommendation that is sometimes given is to tell other people about your long-term goal. This provides a new immediate consequence that supports the long-term goal. However, we have to be aware that when we make a resolution to ourselves or to other people, we usually do so in a moment of cool rationality when we are not under the spell of the temptation.

- Research shows that the mere presence of a temptation activates urges or motives to indulge in the undesired behavior. For example, for people who are dieting, food cues—such as seeing food or even smelling food—cause them to report greater hunger and a great desire to eat.

- People are often surprised when their strong intentions to control themselves suddenly fail when temptations arise, but that's because their intention was made when the temptations weren't present. People who are successful at self-control plan ahead to avoid strong temptations because they know that they might not be able to resist the urge after it arises.

- Research on how children resist temptation shows that even by age four, some children have developed useful self-control strategies. In one series of studies, psychologist Walter Mischel and his colleagues showed children a tray of goodies such as marshmallows, cookies, and pretzel sticks and asked each child which one they liked the most.

- Then, the researcher made each child an offer: They could either eat one treat right away, or if they waited for a few minutes, they could have two treats. The child was then left alone for 20 minutes with a treat, which he or she could eat at any time—but then would not receive a second treat.

- Children showed a lot of variability in how they dealt with this temptation: Some ate the treat immediately, some waited awhile but then gave in, and some held out for the whole 20 minutes and got two treats. In many cases, the children who resisted the treat covered up their eyes or turned their chairs around so they couldn't see the goodies.

- The first line of defense in resisting temptations is to avoid being exposed to them. Sometimes that's not possible, but when you can just stay away from a temptation, do it.

- Research also tells us that once people are being tempted, they aren't likely to control themselves unless they are thinking consciously about their goals at the time. Whatever your goals and values are, you don't just pursue them automatically unless you have developed very strong habits. Often, you must be consciously thinking about those goals or values in order to act consistently with them.

- Of course, keeping your goal in mind doesn't always help. People sometimes engage in undesired behaviors even while they are telling themselves that they shouldn't be doing it. These are called **akratic actions**, a term that comes from a Greek word that means a failure of will or self-control. Akratic actions show that although keeping one's goal in mind is necessary for self-control, it isn't always sufficient.

**Many people try to watch their weight, but they sometimes are tempted by dessert and cannot control themselves.**

- Another reason that we fail at self-control is that our primary goals change. We are often balancing competing goals in a dual-motive conflict, and if the relative importance or salience of the goals change, our actions may change. When people fail at self-control with respect to one goal, they may be very successful with respect to the competing goal.

**Self-Control Strength**

- Over the past 15 years, psychological researchers have become very interested in a previously unexamined aspect of self-control—the idea that it takes a certain amount of psychological energy to make ourselves do what we should and not do what we shouldn't. Sometimes, we just don't seem to have enough of whatever that energy is. Researchers who study this topic call this energy **self-control strength** or self-regulatory resources.

- Researchers have had trouble identifying precisely what self-control strength or willpower is, so they've resorted to metaphors. Some researchers think of it as operating like a muscle. To lift something heavy, your muscles have to be strong enough, and to exert self-control requires that your will is strong enough—that you have enough self-control strength.

- Other people think of it as functioning like a battery. Just as a battery can become too weak to power a flashlight or cell phone, your self-control battery can be too weak to control your impulses and behavior.

- People sometimes feel that they don't have enough self-control strength to do something. For example, some people might say that they can't make themselves get out of bed in the morning or that they just can't make themselves exercise. These are interesting claims because these people are saying that they can't control their own actions.

- What would happen to the person who can't get out of bed in the morning if his or her bedroom were set on fire? Would the person have enough energy to get out of bed? What if the person who just can't exercise were offered $50,000 if he or she exercises five days a week for a year?

- Sometimes, it genuinely feels like we can't control ourselves—that we can't resist a temptation or make ourselves do what we should— but it's usually not actually true.

- We sometimes have more of this mysterious self-control energy than at other times, and it does sometimes feel like we lack it altogether. Sometimes, it is easy to control yourself, but then something changes, and you just don't have what it takes to resist the temptations anymore.

- Studies have shown that when people must control their behavior on one task, their ability to control themselves on a second task is then weakened. For example, research participants might be asked to watch a video of a woman talking and be told to ignore words that appear at the bottom of the screen, or they might watch a comedian and be told to suppress any signs of amusement that they might feel.

- Then, after doing one of these tasks that require self-control, participants are asked to do a different self-control task—to focus on a boring task or to suppress their emotional reactions to upsetting photographs.

- Consistently, participants who perform one task that requires self-control do more poorly on a second self-control task than participants who hadn't done an initial self-control task. Perhaps the first task used up some of their self-control strength so that they didn't have enough for the second task.

- Researchers have been careful to eliminate other possible explanations of these effects. For example, studies show that the effects are not due to changes in emotion or to general fatigue; they seem to be due specifically to depletion of self-control resources.

- This effect has also been shown with dogs. In one interesting study, a researcher used a dog that would obediently sit and wait when its food was served until it was told to eat. Sometimes, the researcher made the dog sit and wait awhile, but at other times, the researcher didn't make the dog wait very long.

- Then, after having to wait or not having to wait and then being allowed to eat, the dog was given a toy that required persistence to open in order to get a treat. Dogs that made themselves wait longer for the food seemed to have less self-control strength—less willpower—to work on another task than dogs who didn't have to control themselves earlier.

- If you monitor yourself closely, you'll notice that your self-control strength waxes and wanes. Sometimes, you have a lot of self-control, but at other times, you don't have enough control to make yourself do something that you should do or to keep yourself from doing something that you shouldn't do.

- For most people, self-control strength decreases as the day continues. By the end of the day, many people have been engaging in a lot of self-control for many hours—sometimes to the point that their self-control strength is pretty low. This is not just a matter of physical fatigue; it's the depletion of self-control strength.

## Important Terms

**akratic action**: The undesired behavior that people sometimes engage in while they are telling themselves that they shouldn't be engaging in the behavior; comes from a Greek word that means a failure of will or self-control.

**dual-motive conflict**: A conflict between two competing goals or motives.

**self-control strength**: The psychological energy it takes to make people do what they should and not do what they shouldn't.

**temporal discounting**: The notion that people discount outcomes that are further away in time.

## Suggested Reading

Baumeister and Tierney, *Willpower.*

Westerhoff, "Set in Our Ways."

## Questions to Consider

1. What is a dual-motive conflict, and how are dual-motive conflicts involved in self-regulation failures?

2. What evidence do we have that controlling our behavior requires a special source of energy, or self-control strength, that is temporarily depleted by acts of self-control?

# Why Do We Forget?
## Lecture 12

H uman memory is a genuinely amazing feature of our brains. We often complain about our memories—that we forgot an appointment or someone's birthday or where we put our car keys—but we have to consider those lapses in memory alongside the hundreds of thousands of things we do remember each day. Furthermore, we can pull information out of our memories very quickly and usually without error. However, we all experience times in which our memories fail us—and often in puzzling ways. In this lecture, you will learn the various reasons that we forget.

**The Trace Decay Theory of Forgetting**

- In everyday language, we use the word "forget" anytime we can't recall something that we think we should know, but in many cases, our inability to recall something doesn't involve forgetting—it was never committed to our memory to begin with. Cognitive psychologists call these instances encoding failures. Often, we don't encode information about something, so it's simply not in memory when we try to retrieve it later.

- At one time, you might have known a historical fact, a piece of trivia, or a certain person's name—showing that the information was in your memory—but you may discover that the information has slipped away, perhaps forever.

- **Cognitive psychologists**, the scientists who study thinking and memory, have offered two general types of explanations for why we forget: that something has happened to a memory trace—it has decayed or deteriorated over time, making the memory difficult or impossible to retrieve—or that the information is still in the brain, but something is interfering with the person's ability to retrieve it.

- According to **trace decay theory**, a memory trace is created every time a new memory is formed. You can think of this trace as a strengthening of connections in the brain that help to maintain that memory.

- Scientists don't have a complete picture of how memories are stored in the brain. They have identified the primary areas of the brain that are involved in memory, and they understand some of the changes that occur to individual neurons and brain circuits when we remember.

- Although we don't understand all of the physiological details, we can still talk loosely about some sort of memory trace being laid down when we remember things. The trace decay theory of forgetting suggests that things can happen that cause these memory traces to fade or disappear.

- Some researchers believe that the mere passage of time can cause a memory trace to decay. If information is not retrieved—that is, remembered—from time to time, the memory trace will become weaker and weaker until it fades away entirely, and you can't remember the information.

## Other Explanations of Forgetting

- As plausible as trace decay explanations of forgetting seem, they have a number of problems, and many cognitive scientists do not think that simple memory decay plays much of a role in forgetting.

- One problem is that many memories that have not been rehearsed or remembered remain remarkably strong and stable for a very long time. In fact, some studies have shown that people can sometimes remember things later on that they were not able to remember earlier, which argues against the idea that memories naturally decay.

- Researchers have found trace decay theory difficult to test in controlled experiments. The problem is that as time goes by, not only is there time for a memory trace to decay as the theory suggests, but there are also opportunities for new memories that we form to interfere with older memories. There's no way to allow a period of time for memories to decay without opening the possibility that new experiences are interfering with older memories.

- If memories weaken over time, then we don't know whether forgetting is due to a decay of the memory trace or to other things that are happening. No one can say for certain that memories don't naturally decay over time, but researchers don't consider decay to be an important process in most everyday forgetting.

- Whether memory traces decay over time or not, it certainly appears that memory traces can be disturbed at the time that memories are being encoded in the brain. Whenever we take in new information, our brain needs time to make permanent changes to store the memory properly. This process is called memory consolidation. If events interfere with this consolidation process, the memory trace will be weak—or the memory won't be stored at all.

- A second explanation of forgetting suggests that the information that you want to remember is still stored in memory, but something has interfered with your ability to retrieve it.

- Memories can compete and interfere with each other, making them difficult to remember. Interference across memories is particularly likely when information in one memory is very similar to information in other memories.

- The idea behind interference is that as you learn new information, new material sometimes interferes either with older things that you once knew or with future things that you might learn later. It can get mixed up in memory, with old and new memories interfering with each other.

- Another explanation is that forgetting occurs when there isn't a suitable retrieval cue to trigger the memory. Memories don't always come to consciousness spontaneously on their own; a cue is often needed to bring them out. Research has shown that we have much more in our memory than we can often retrieve, and having the right cue to trigger the memory is often all that is needed.

## Motivated Forgetting and Repressed Memories

- There is a controversial explanation for forgetting that involves the possibility that people sometimes forget things because they are motivated to forget them. Some researchers have suggested that people may actively work to repress memories—especially memories that are traumatic or disturbing. In motivated forgetting, people genuinely forget things that they want to forget, but the notion of repressed memories is very controversial.

- Repressed memories have received a lot of attention in the context of childhood sexual abuse. Many psychotherapists claim that their patients have recalled previously repressed memories of horrible events that they had pushed into their unconscious, but there are several problems with the idea of repressed memories.

- First, there's virtually no research evidence to support the idea that repression even occurs. It's been tremendously difficult to study repressed memories because it's usually impossible to verify that the recovered memory is accurate, and even if we know that the disturbing event really happened, it's not clear how we would ever show whether the event had been repressed as opposed to merely forgotten.

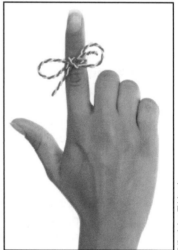

© iStockphoto/Thinkstock.

- In addition, people certainly do remember horrible things that happened to them. In fact, research suggests that most

**Sometimes, when we try to remember something but can't, it's because the memory was never encoded in the first place.**

victims of traumatic events remember the event too often and in too much detail. The idea that people regularly repress memories of trauma is simply not true.

- Furthermore, many cases of recovered repressed memories have been shown to be false, and others are very unlikely to have actually happened.

- Additionally, many of our normal, everyday memories are not accurate. Given that normal, nontraumatic memories are subject to distortions, there's no reason to think that repressed memories are any more accurate.

- People who have experienced traumatic events sometimes do forget about them for a while, and it is possible that certain memories might actually be repressed, but there are so many questions and contradictions surrounding repressed memories that there's no way to know what's really going on in any particular case in which someone claims to have recalled a repressed memory. Given that uncertainty, we must be very careful about the idea of repressed memories until we know much more about them.

## Flashbulb Memories and Remembering

- We all forget most of what happens to us, but some memories seem to be etched so deeply into our minds that it would seem impossible to ever forget them. Psychologists use the term **flashbulb memories** to describe very detailed, exceptionally vivid memories of the circumstances in which you heard surprising, important, or emotionally arousing news.

- Initially, cognitive psychologists thought that flashbulb memories were a special type of memory that was immune to forgetting, but research suggests they may not be all that different from other memories. A number of studies suggest that flashbulb memories are not especially accurate—even though they are quite vivid and people are more confident that they are true.

- Researchers have studied these memories by asking people to describe a flashbulb memory—for example, of the U.S. space shuttle *Challenger* explosion or of the 9/11 terrorist attacks—soon after the event occurred. Then, several months or even years later, they ask the same participants to describe the memory again.

- In most cases, people's memories of the details of the situation change, often in dramatic ways. However, people remain certain that the memory is very accurate—even though a lot of forgetting and interference can occur. Therefore, our most vivid and important memories are subject to forgetting and distortion.

- Most people think of memory as a video recorder that records an experience and then plays it back later. However, research shows that memory does not work that way; instead, memories are reconstructed each time you recall them, pulled together in bits and pieces.

- When people try to retrieve information about a particular event, a few highlights of the episode come immediately to mind—but not all of the details. Then, people reconstruct the rest of the episode from the bits and pieces of the memory that they do have, adding other information so that the memory makes sense.

- Human remembering is often a process of reconstructing what must have happened rather than directly recalling what did happen. The result is that the memories we recall are often distorted.

- Much of the time, memory distortions don't matter much, but in some instances, distorted or false memories can have major consequences. The topic of false memories is of particular interest in the context of eyewitness testimony. False memories have sent innocent people to prison and even to death row.

- Like repressed memories, eyewitness identification is fraught with problems, and research evidence strongly suggests that we should not place much emphasis on the memories of eyewitnesses.

Unfortunately, research also shows that juries place a lot of credence on what eyewitnesses say that they saw—even when they are remembering something that happened months or years ago.

- Many cognitive psychologists think that the reconstructive and even imperfect nature of memory is actually a benefit. Although forgetting sometimes creates problems for us, it is actually a very important and adaptive feature of the human brain.

- The brain appears designed to allow unused memories to become less accessible. Memory systems probably evolved to provide us with access to information that helps us deal with the situations that we often encounter and to help us plan for the future—not so that we could remember everything that we ever learned or experienced.

- For most practical purposes, it is not useful to maintain detailed memories of everything indefinitely. This isn't a problem with the system; it's absolutely essential so that we are not overwhelmed with memories that are unimportant or that interfere with new information.

## Important Terms

**cognitive psychologist**: A scientist who studies thinking and memory.

**flashbulb memory**: A very detailed, exceptionally vivid memory of the circumstances in which a person heard surprising, important, or emotionally arousing news.

**trace decay theory**: A theory that claims that a memory trace, which strengthens the connections in the brain that help to maintain a memory, is created every time a new memory is formed.

## Suggested Reading

Higbee, *Your Memory*.

Law, "Seared in Our Memories."

## Questions to Consider

1. Does research suggest that forgetting is due more to the decay of memory traces or to interference from other memories? Explain your answer.

2. Why do experts who study memory urge caution when it comes to the idea of repressed memories?

# Can Subliminal Messages Affect Behavior?
## Lecture 13

W  e are constantly affected by things that we are unaware of, but that's not quite the same as knowing whether we are influenced by stimuli that are presented to us below our level of awareness or whether someone else could influence what we decide to do without our knowledge by presenting us with subliminal stimuli. Certainly, conscious awareness isn't necessary in order for a human being to respond to its environment. In fact, subliminal stimuli can affect people's thoughts, emotions, and behaviors, but the effects are rather limited.

**Effects of Subliminal Stimuli**

- A **subliminal stimulus** is a stimulus that cannot consciously be perceived. For example, if a word or picture is flashed on a computer screen for only 40 milliseconds, you won't see it—at least not consciously—but the question is whether the information in that word or picture gets into your brain anyway, without you consciously detecting it. If it does, the question becomes whether that subliminal word or picture can affect what you think, feel, or do.

- Before the past century, not only did we not have any way to present a stimulus for only a fraction of a second, but if people couldn't report what they experienced—because it's subliminal—we would need some high-tech equipment to measure whatever effect the subliminal stimulus might have on people. Researchers in cognitive and social psychology now have this kind of equipment, so we're learning a great deal about the effects of subliminal stimuli.

- There's no question that we are affected by things that we aren't consciously aware of. You constantly think and do things without having any idea what the stimuli were that led you to think or do them—and you are certainly not aware of the processes inside your brain that lead to your thoughts or behavior.

- However, that's not quite the same as asking the question of whether we are influenced by stimuli that are presented to us below our level of awareness, and it doesn't answer the question of whether someone else could influence what we decide without our knowledge by presenting us with subliminal stimuli.

- One way to answer these questions is to study people's emotional reactions to subliminal stimuli by flashing negative or positive photographs too quickly for participants to see and then by measuring the effects of the pictures on their emotions.

- In fact, subliminal photographs can produce very distinct emotions. In various studies, flashing disgusting pictures subliminally increased participants' feelings of disgust and flashing frightening pictures increased participants' feelings of fear.

- The effects of subliminal stimuli can go beyond simply making people feel good or bad. For example, graduate students at the University of Michigan were presented with either a photograph of their scowling department chairman or a photograph of a smiling person. These pictures were flashed for only two milliseconds, and none of the participants reported seeing anything when they were asked.

- Then, the graduate students evaluated one of their own research ideas, rating how original and important the idea was. Results showed that the students rated their research ideas significantly more negatively if they had been exposed to the disapproving scowl of their department chair than if they had been exposed to the smiling face. A two-millisecond flash of a photograph that they didn't see influenced their ratings of themselves and their ideas.

- Research suggests that subliminal stimuli are processed at a pretty deep level; that is, even though participants don't consciously see pictures, their brains can extract the identity of a person in a picture and even the nature of his or her expression. In addition, subliminal photographs can affect not only our emotions in general, but also how we evaluate ourselves.

- There's an interesting application of this phenomenon that's being discussed among experts in this area, and that involves using subliminal tests for lie detection. In the future, it might be possible to flash a picture of a house that a thief supposedly broke into and see what sort of reaction the thief has.

**Conscious versus Nonconscious Stimuli**
- If subliminal stimuli can influence our emotional responses, think about what might happen if a person sees one stimulus consciously while another one is shown nonconsciously, or subliminally. Research suggests that it is possible that the subliminal stimulus that you can't see can influence your judgment of the stimuli that you can see.

- In an early demonstration of this effect, researchers told participants that they would be rating how much they liked a set of Chinese **ideographs**, which are characters or symbols that represent objects and ideas. The participants didn't know that right before they saw each ideograph, a photograph of either a smiling face or an angry face was flashed for four milliseconds—too fast to be detected consciously.

- Participants rated the ideographs that followed subliminal smiling faces more positively than the ideographs that followed subliminal angry faces. Of course, the participants naturally assumed that they actually liked or disliked a particular ideograph, not knowing that their reactions were caused by the subliminal smiling or angry face.

- Such a process could potentially be used to influence people's attitudes toward products or political candidates, for example. These results suggest that if happy pictures were flashed subliminally before you saw a new brand of breakfast cereal, it might lead you to feel good about the cereal.

- In the Chinese ideograph study, the visual stimulus—the one that people could see consciously—was relatively neutral. In other words, people don't feel strongly about ideographs. Because they didn't have any preexisting feelings about the things that they were evaluating, the weak emotions created by the subliminal stimulus—the smiling or angry subliminal face—could influence participants' ratings.

- Furthermore, although the subliminal stimuli—the smiling and angry faces—caused people to rate the ideographs differently, the sizes of the effects were rather small.

**Popcorn and soda sales might increase when subliminal messages are flashed to an audience that is already hungry and thirsty.**

- Subliminal effects are real, but they are probably not strong enough to influence people's evaluations of things that they already have strong attitudes about—such as real products or politicians.

## Subliminal Stimuli and Behavior

- Under certain circumstances, subliminal stimuli can influence our emotions and preferences, and they can affect how we feel about things that we perceive consciously. In addition, although the effects appear to be confined to relatively simple behaviors, subliminal stimuli can influence our actual behavior.

- For example, several research studies have shown that we can increase thirst and hunger by subliminally presenting participants with words that connote being thirsty or hungry.

- Studies have also shown that subliminal words that are associated with the stereotypes of certain social groups lead people to act more like they think people in those groups act.

- In one study, participants were shown a list of words, and researchers wanted to know whether subliminally priming stereotypes that are associated with older people caused participants to remember fewer words—because forgetfulness is often associated with older people.

- Participants who were subliminally primed with words that are associated with stereotypes about the elderly remembered significantly fewer words, especially if they had a lot of contact with older people in their everyday lives.

- This study and similar experiments show that subliminal stimuli can affect not only our emotions but also how we respond to other people. In fact, this seems to be one way that subliminal influences creep into our everyday behavior.

- Things happen around us that we're not consciously processing, yet these subliminal events can steer our thoughts in particular directions, influencing our emotions and behavior—but it's a very subtle process.

- In order to affect people, a subliminal stimulus must be relatively simple—a couple of words or an image—and it must be presented in such a way that it can't be consciously detected.

- In addition, it helps if there's not much else going on in the situation that the person is in; it's probably easier to get these effects in a quiet research laboratory than in the hustle and bustle of everyday life.

- Once the subliminal stimulus is registered mentally, it's usually not going to cause a particular behavior—just certain emotional inclinations and mental associations.

- A recent study showed that subliminal priming will affect people's behavior only if the subliminal stimulus is relevant to a goal that the person already has.

- For example, if you're not thirsty, subliminal messages aren't going to cause you to buy a soda, but if you're already thirsty, a subliminal message might influence your choice. Therefore, presenting a subliminal message involving a particular brand of soft drink might cause that brand to come more easily to your mind when you do decide to drink something.

## Subliminal Audio Stimuli

- Subliminal audio stimuli are sound waves that cannot be heard consciously. The notion of subliminal audio stimuli forms the basis of the 50-million-dollar industry that makes self-help audio recordings that contain subliminal messages. There are recorded programs to help people lose weight, improve memory, and enhance self-esteem by using subliminal audio messages that are imbedded either in music or in relaxing sounds such as white noise or ocean surf.

- Several controlled experiments have been conducted to test the effectiveness of subliminal recordings in helping people with various problems, and they uniformly fail to find any evidence that audio programs containing subliminal suggestions are effective.

- There are several reasons that recorded subliminal messages don't help people. First, research suggests that in order to influence emotions or behavior, information in subliminal messages must be very simple—only a couple of words at most. However, these self-help recordings usually contain entire sentences—and many of them.

- There are studies showing that words that are subliminally hidden in babble can sometimes influence people's reactions and choices, but the message must be very simple.

- Second, the subliminal messages are often covered up by music or background noise. The brain must be able to separate the message from the other sounds, and there's no evidence that it can separate the subliminal audio track from the louder music or background noise in these recordings.

- Finally, there's nothing that says that every message that the brain receives will automatically have its intended effect. It's one thing to demonstrate that a subliminal picture of an angry face might have an emotional impact on a participant in a study, but it's quite another to claim that subliminal messages will lead to long-term behavior changes associated with losing weight or improving memory.

- Research suggests that subliminal stimuli that are presented visually are more likely to affect behavior than auditory subliminal messages.

- Many people are surprised to learn that subliminal stimuli can affect us in many ways, but it shouldn't be surprising if you consider the fact that your brain doesn't usually care whether a piece of information is received subliminally or in conscious awareness. As long as the stimulus or information reaches the brain, it's there. Whether you happened to be consciously aware of it is irrelevant.

## Important Terms

**ideograph**: A character or symbol that represents an object or an idea.

**subliminal stimulus**: A stimulus that cannot consciously be perceived.

## Suggested Reading

Hassin, Uleman, and Bargh, eds., *The New Unconscious*.

Wilson, *Strangers to Ourselves*.

1. What evidence do we have that subliminal stimuli can affect people's emotions and self-evaluations?

2. Why is it unlikely that people's attitudes toward important topics can be changed by using subliminal messages in everyday life?

# Why Do We Dream?

## Lecture 14

Dreams are often a combination of rather normal and commonplace events paired with occasional nonsense. Much of our dreams are linked loosely to the people, places, and things that we know while also containing many fictional elements mixed with fantasy. Researchers have offered many reasonable explanations of why people dream, but none of them are entirely consistent with the data that research has provided about sleep and dreaming. Perhaps that means that we haven't yet uncovered the real purpose of dreaming, or maybe it means that dreaming doesn't actually have a function—or maybe we're just asking the wrong questions.

### Sleeping and Dreaming

- Each night, we pass through a series of stages of sleep, each of which is associated with a distinctive pattern of brain waves. In a normal night's sleep, we cycle through the various stages of sleep several times—usually between four and six times—and each of these cycles includes one stage of **rapid eye movement (REM) sleep**, or dreaming sleep. Therefore, on an average night, each of us dreams on four to six separate occasions.

- The first episode of REM sleep usually occurs about 90 minutes after we fall asleep, and it's relatively short. With each new cycle of sleep stages, the time that we spend in REM becomes increasingly longer. Therefore, we do most of our dreaming as morning approaches. Over the course of an average night, we spend about a quarter of our sleeping time in REM sleep, which is far more than researchers once believed.

- Scientists have proposed many explanations of dreaming, and many of those explanations have some degree of research support, but all of them have conceptual problems or are inconsistent with various research evidence.

- Sigmund Freud was one of the first people to discuss the purpose of dreaming in detail, and his perspective dominated work on dreaming for many years. Freud's psychoanalytic theory suggested that dreams reflect people's unconscious thoughts and desires.

- According to Freud, most of our behavior centers around basic sexual and aggressive impulses that have to be fulfilled if people are to be healthy and happy, but because society constrains people from acting on these impulses, they push awareness of these urges out of their conscious mind. Freud thought that these wishes and desires still needed to be expressed, so they show up in our dreams.

- Freud admitted that as you think about your dreams, it might not be obvious to you that most of them deal with satisfying your desires for sex and aggression, but that's because your unconscious mind disguises the meaning of your dreams so that you won't be upset by how disturbing they are.

- Decades of research have failed to support Freud's views of dreaming. Some practicing psychoanalysts continue to operate as if Freud's wish fulfillment theory of dreams were true, but virtually none of Freud's claims about the nature of dreams have been confirmed by empirical research.

## Dream Theories

- Modern researchers suggest that it's possible that the brain activity associated with REM sleep is doing something important—that it has some biological function—but that the actual dreams that we experience may not do anything at all.

- Many researchers have suggested that the existence of such a complex brain process as REM sleep—in both mammals and birds—indicates that it's probably very important. This particular stage of sleep seems to do something that's necessary for well-being and survival because animals that are deprived of REM sleep become very disturbed and may eventually die.

- However, even if the brain activity associated with REM sleep is vitally important, the actual dreams that we experience may be just a by-product of those brain states and don't do anything in their own right.

- **Activation-synthesis theory** is the first modern theory of dreams that is still accepted by many dream researchers. The main idea behind this theory is that dreams are the brain's efforts to make sense out of meaningless patterns of firing in the brain as we sleep.

- According to this theory, our dreams are often disjointed and strange because higher cognitive areas of the brain are trying to interpret signals that are just by-products of activity going on in other parts of the brain.

- Activation-synthesis theory has enjoyed a lot of scientific acceptance, but research evidence for it is somewhat mixed, and the theory says relatively little about why our dreams have the content that they do.

- Other theories of dreams, however, suggest that dreams are functional—that they do something useful. One functional theory suggests that dreams help people to solve personal problems by finding solutions to things in life that are bothering them.

- The problem-solving explanation for dreaming sounds plausible, but it doesn't agree with much research either. For example, less than half of the dreams that people report have any connection—however remote—to the events they experienced the previous day, and even far fewer seem to have anything to do with people's current problems.

- Furthermore, the fact that people recall only a very small percentage of their dreams also argues against the problem-solving theory. It wouldn't make much sense to have a process that helped us figure out solutions to our problems but that didn't allow us to remember the solutions that dreaming provided.

- If dreams help with our problems, then it would seem that people who remember their dreams would be at a great advantage in life compared to people who don't recall many of their dreams each night, but research doesn't show differences in well-being between people who do and do not remember their dreams.

- Other theories of dreaming focus on what the brain is doing when people dream, and these explanations don't require that people remember their dreams in order for the process to be beneficial.

- For example, one theory suggests that dreams are involved in the process of cleaning up recent memories and other clutter from the mind. The images in our dreams are just snippets of memories that are being scanned and evaluated for deletion, thereby cleaning the mind to prepare for the next day.

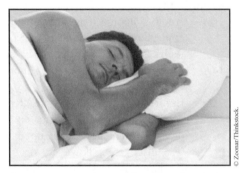

**A person may not remember dreaming, but sleep research shows that everyone dreams every night.**

- Like the other theories, the cleanup explanation makes sense, but not everything that we know about dreaming supports it. Only about half of our dreams involve anything related to our recent experiences, so it's not clear that our dreams reflect recent memories that are being scanned and deleted.

- In addition, the cleanup explanation would seem to predict that our dreams would be composed of piecemeal snippets of memories, but they usually aren't. Dreams often have an internally consistent story line that doesn't have any obvious connection to anything that actually happened to us recently.

- A similar explanation known as **consolidation theory** suggests that dreams are involved in the storage of memories from the previous day. Memories undergo a process of consolidation that helps to store them in long-term memory, and some researchers believe that dreaming occurs each night during the consolidation process.

- This is another explanation in which the content of a dream is just a by-product of brain activity that's occurring as memories are consolidated. This explanation has many of the same problems as the cleanup theory. When researchers analyze the content of people's dreams, they don't often seem to involve actual memories—as the theory would predict.

**Dream Content**
- Another approach to understanding dreaming is to examine the content of people's dreams. People tend to dream about certain topics far more than other topics, so perhaps the uncommon, strange dreams can tell us something about the person who has them.

- Before we knew that people dream mostly during a special stage of sleep, researchers had to rely mostly on people reporting their dreams when they woke up in the morning. Once REM sleep was discovered, however, sleep researchers could wake people up during REM sleep and almost always get a report of a dream in progress.

- Many of these studies examined the question of whether the content of people's dreams is affected by things that happen to them either right before they go to sleep or during the REM state itself. Researchers have concluded that the content of our dreams is not affected much by what's going on around us at the time.

- The relatively few occasions in which people incorporate stimuli from their environment into their dreams are interesting because they show how quickly and ingeniously the brain fits those stimuli into dreams that are already in progress.

- Other studies have been conducted in which people's dreams are compared to the things that actually happen in their everyday lives, and these studies show that there is continuity between the content of people's dreams and their waking lives.

- People rarely have dreams about other people or events that don't pertain to them. Most dreams are not just weird, random patterns of thoughts; they often involve themes that are important to us.

- In fact, studies show that—contrary to the belief that dreams are mostly bizarre and unrealistic—most dreams involve realistic life situations. Even when dreams involve fictional scenarios, people engage in normal human behaviors.

## Bizarre Dreams and Nightmares

- Most of what happens in our dreams is rather ordinary, but sometimes dreams do contain some pretty strange material. Some researchers suggest that much of the strangeness that we experience in dreams is due to the use of metaphors.

- Much of our thought in everyday life is metaphorical, and it seems that metaphors creep into our dreams as well. When metaphors are expressed in dreams, they can generate bizarre images because while dreaming, we interpret them literally.

- In dreams, verbal metaphors can become visual. There's probably nothing symbolic about these kinds of images. They are just visual images for metaphors that are interpreted literally when parts of the brain that normally distinguish literal from figurative language shut down during sleep.

- Another reason that parts of dreams are nonsensical—and that we don't even notice how strange they are at the time—is that certain areas of the brain that are responsible for reality testing and critical judgment are deactivated during REM sleep, leading to illogical and unrealistic thinking.

- Although dreams deal with many of the same themes as people's thoughts when they are awake, dreams are more negative than waking life. People report more threatening events, misfortunes, and negative emotions in their dreams than they actually experience in their lives.

- Researchers have debated the question of whether nightmares are just severely bad dreams or whether they are a qualitatively different phenomenon. Dream researchers define **nightmares** as dreams that are very vivid, involve strong negative emotions such as fear or grief, and wake the person up.

- Research suggests that bad dreams that do not wake people up can sometimes be more intense than nightmares, so it's not clear that using wakening as an index of the severity of a dream is a good idea. Research also shows that nightmares are associated with stressful events in people's lives, and nightmares increase when people are under stress.

- As with dreams, the question arises of whether nightmares serve any function or whether they merely disrupt sleep and make people miserable, and the answer is that we don't know.

## Important Terms

**activation-synthesis theory**: The first modern theory of dreams that suggests that dreams are the brain's efforts to make sense out of meaningless patterns of firing in the brain while sleeping.

**consolidation theory**: A theory of dreams that suggests that dreams are involved in the storage of memories from the previous day.

**nightmare**: A dream that is very vivid, involves strong negative emotions such as fear or grief, and wakes a person up.

**rapid eye movement (REM) sleep**: The stage of sleep that occurs once per cycle—and between four and six times per night—that is characterized by dreaming sleep.

## Suggested Reading

Hobson, *Dreaming*.

Rock, *The Mind at Night*.

## Questions to Consider

1. How did the discovery of REM sleep revolutionize the study of dreaming?

2. Describe the explanations of dreaming that are based on each of the following: activation synthesis, problem solving, cleanup, and consolidation.

# Why Are People So Full of Themselves?
## Lecture 15

Almost everybody is inherently egotistical and prone to an assortment of self-serving biases, which cause people to view themselves more positively than objective evidence suggests that they should. We deceive ourselves because it makes us feel better than seeing the truth; we can feel good about being better than average even if we're not. Self-serving biases are widespread, and we generally think of them as being normal. In this lecture, you'll learn why people tend to think that they are better than they are and how people's views of themselves affect others.

**Self-Serving Biases**
- Studies have shown that the vast majority of people think that they are better than average on most positive characteristics. However, most abilities and psychological characteristics are roughly normally distributed, which means that they fall into a bell-shaped distribution with an equal number of people falling below the average and falling above average.

- This better-than-average effect is just one example of what psychologists call **self-serving biases**, or egotistical biases, which revolve around the notion that most people think that they are better than they actually are. Sometimes people see themselves more negatively than they should, but when people err in their judgments of themselves, they tend to err in the positive direction.

- Not only do people think that they are better than average, but they also think that the things that are associated with them are better than average—even if they admit that they're not the very best. People tend to think that their groups, friends, children, personal values, and alma maters are better than those of other people.

- A strange example of this phenomenon is the **mere ownership effect**, which refers to the fact that merely owning something makes people view it as better and more valuable. People overvalue things that they own because we obtain and buy things that we think are good.

- For example, when researchers ask people to rate how much they like the letters of the alphabet, they tend to rate their own initials higher than chance. The name-letter effect shows how invested we can be in things that are associated with us. Not only do people evaluate the letters of their initials favorably, but they also evaluate things that have those letters more favorably.

- A series of studies showed that people tend to gravitate to states and cities that resemble their own names. However, it is also possible that parents tend to give their children names that resemble the state or city they are born in. Researchers have done their best to test other explanations, but they don't explain the name-letter effect. People actually move to cities and states that resemble their names at a disproportionate rate—without being aware that they're doing so.

- In addition, people often try to excuse their shortcomings and failures while claiming responsibility for the good things that happen. Hundreds of studies have shown that the attributions that people make tend to be biased in ways that portray them in a positive light.

- When people perform well, they tend to say that they did well because they're smart or they tried hard—their good performance was due to something about their own ability or effort. However, when they perform poorly and things go wrong, people tend to say that it wasn't their fault.

- It's difficult for us to see the biases that we all have in favor of ourselves because we naturally believe that our own beliefs about ourselves are true. In addition, we each think that we see ourselves more accurately than most other people see themselves.

## The Benefits and Drawbacks of Self-Serving Biases

- The question of whether self-serving biases are beneficial or harmful has been a controversial issue among research psychologists. One side suggests that it's healthy and helpful to maintain positive illusions about oneself, which create positive emotions and helps people stay motivated when they encounter setbacks and difficulties.

- The other side agrees that people feel better when they evaluate themselves more positively than they should, but they argue that there are some fairly large costs to these biases—both for the person and for the people around him or her.

- Presumably, people manage their lives better when they see their abilities and personal characteristics accurately than when their views of themselves are distorted—in either a positive or a negative direction. Overestimating one's personal ability or skill can lead people to pursue goals that are beyond their ability and set them up for failure.

- People who overestimate their capabilities are likely to get themselves into situations that they aren't able to handle. Additionally, overly positive self-views can deter people from doing things to correct problems or improve themselves.

- Although it's true that seeing oneself too positively might lead people to persevere when they hit obstacles and setbacks in life, it doesn't make much sense to keep trying to do things that are beyond one's ability. It seems much more adaptive to understand one's limits.

- Research also suggests that self-serving biases can damage our relationships with other people. A lot of conflict with other people comes about because most of us think that we're better than average and that we're right most of the time.

- You can see this effect when people work together in groups—such as on committees, teams, decision-making groups, and work groups. Because each person in the group thinks that he or she is better than the average group member, each person interprets what happens in the group through the eyes of his or her self-serving bias.

- Therefore, when the group does well on some task, each member tends to take too much personal credit for how well things went. Each person thinks that his or her contribution to the group's success was greater than the average member's contribution.

- However, when the group does poorly, each person takes too little responsibility for the group's failure. Each person thinks that his or her contribution was better than average, so they aren't as responsible for whatever went wrong as most of the other group members were.

- Both of these patterns can lead to conflict in a group. In the case of a successful group, each person feels that the other members aren't giving him or her quite enough credit. Conflicts can emerge in successful groups because each person feels more responsible for the success than he or she should. Furthermore, each member is irked if he or she realizes that other members are taking more credit than they deserve.

- In a failing group, each person feels like the others are shirking responsibility and placing too much blame on him or her. Because an individual thinks that he or she was less responsible for the group's problems than most of the other members, the individual feels that he or she is being blamed more than is deserved.

## Self-Serving Biases and Self-Esteem
- Historically, the most common answer to why people think that they are better than they are has been that people inflate their self-views because they have a need for high self-esteem, but it's not clear that people actually have a need for self-esteem. There's not

much evidence that human beings have a built-in need just to feel good about themselves.

- Of course, judging oneself positively feels good, and thinking that you have positive characteristics makes you feel better than thinking that you have negative characteristics. It reduces people's anxiety and apprehension to think that they have certain abilities or possess positive characteristics that will promote their success and lead other people to like and accept them.

Much of the conflict that occurs in groups exists because most people believe that they are better than average.

- Our beliefs about ourselves are there to help guide our behavior in adaptive ways, but because we can change how we feel by changing how we think, we can create positive feelings and avoid negative feelings by thinking about ourselves in unrealistically positive ways. Because people have the capacity for self-awareness and self-evaluation, they can essentially fool themselves into feeling better than they otherwise would.

- Some self-serving biases are aimed as much at other people as at ourselves. In many ways, we are even more concerned about what other people think of us than we are of what we think of ourselves. In fact, all of us have negative views of ourselves that we work very hard to hide from other people.

- When we take too much credit for success, deny that we were responsible for failure, or overstate our positive characteristics and downplay our bad ones, these often reflect public, self-presentational efforts to be seen by other people in particular ways.

- Self-serving biases often reflect public impression management rather than biased self-beliefs. We all know that we're going to fare better in life if other people perceive us positively rather than negatively, so we claim to have more positive characteristics than we actually do.

- Evidence suggests that people act like they are better than they are for two distinct reasons: to feel better about themselves and to convey more positive impressions of themselves to other people. Almost everyone shows these self-serving biases, but some people show them more than others.

**Narcissism versus Humility**
- People who score high in narcissism view themselves very positively. Narcissists' self-evaluations go beyond just having high self-esteem to believing that they are superior to other people. They also require a lot of attention and admiration from other people and believe that they deserve to be treated specially. Narcissists also tend to exploit other people—presumably because people who are so special have the right to take advantage of others.

- For many years, there's been a controversy about whether narcissists really feel as good about themselves as they appear to on the surface. The common wisdom has been that people who act like narcissists don't actually like themselves at all. In fact, they view themselves quite negatively, and all of their narcissistic posturing is just a defense against deep-seated feelings of inferiority.

- Evidence suggests that there are two distinct types of narcissists: grandiose narcissists and vulnerable narcissists. **Grandiose narcissists** evaluate themselves positively, as their behavior seems to indicate. Grandiose narcissists spend a lot of time promoting their superiority; they brag about their accomplishments and become upset when other people don't seem to realize how wonderful they are.

- On the other hand, **vulnerable narcissists** are fundamentally insecure about themselves. They think that they are unique and deserve to be treated specially, but they are repeatedly disappointed that they don't get the attention and respect that they think they deserve. Vulnerable narcissists often don't come across as narcissistic; in fact, they can seem anxious and withdrawn.

- At the other end of the continuum from narcissists are individuals who score high in humility—those who don't show the normal degree of self-serving biases. Contrary to the popular conception, humble people don't think poorly of themselves or devalue their accomplishments. Instead, they have an unusually accurate view of themselves—and accept themselves that way. In addition, people who are high in humility don't think that being better than other people entitles them to special treatment.

## Important Terms

**grandiose narcissist**: A narcissist that evaluates himself or herself positively, as behavior seems to indicate.

**mere ownership effect**: The notion that merely owning something makes people view it as better and more valuable.

**self-serving bias**: A bias that revolves around the notion that most people think that they are better than they actually are.

**vulnerable narcissist**: A narcissist that is fundamentally insecure about himself or herself.

## Suggested Reading

Leary, *The Curse of the Self.*

Twenge and Campbell, *The Narcissism Epidemic.*

## Questions to Consider

1. Describe each of the following self-serving biases: better-than-average effect, mere ownership effect, and name-letter effect.

2. What are some benefits and drawbacks of holding overly positive views of oneself? Overall, do you think that self-serving biases are generally beneficial or detrimental to people's well-being?

# Do People Have Psychic Abilities?
## Lecture 16

Many people believe that some individuals possess psychic abilities, such as foreseeing the future or reading other people's minds. Of course, many other people believe that such abilities are nonsense. There has been a lot of scientific research on whether people possess psychic powers, or ESP, even though many people assume that this concept could never be studied scientifically. The existence of psychic phenomena, or psi, is a mystery of human behavior that cannot be resolved to everyone's satisfaction at this point in time, but more and better research will hopefully tell us definitively whether psi exists.

### Psychic Phenomena

- The central figure in the development of scientific research on psychic phenomena, or **psi**, was J. B. Rhine, who was recruited to Duke University in 1927 to conduct research in **parapsychology**, the field that studies anomalous psychic experiences such as extra-sensory perception (ESP). Rhine applied the same scientific approaches used in other sciences, including controlled experiments, to test people for psychic abilities.

- In Rhine's studies, he used a special deck of cards—now known as Zener cards—in which each card had one of five symbols on it: a square, a circle, a star, a plus sign, or three wavy lines. The research participant's job was simply to guess which card would come up next in the deck.

- The deck had 25 cards—five cards of each design—so the probability that a person would randomly guess the cards correctly was one out of five, or 20 percent. If chance guessing was involved, the average person would guess five of the 25 cards, or 20 percent, correctly.

- The question was whether some people could predict more than five cards correctly—so many more that it was very unlikely that they were correct due to chance guessing.

- Of course, people can get lucky and guess a higher percentage correctly on the basis of chance alone. Fortunately for Rhine, however, statisticians of his day had been working on ways to determine the probability of getting any particular number of guesses correct on the basis of chance, so he could determine whether a person's correct answers were the result of random guessing or possible psychic ability.

- Rhine occasionally located people who could guess significantly more cards correctly than would be expected by chance. For example, he tested a young man named Hubert Pearce, who guessed so many Zener cards correctly that the chances that his performance was due to random guessing was one in 22 billion. In fact, at one point, Pearce guessed 25 cards correctly in a row. The odds of doing that by random guessing are one in 300 quadrillion.

- Of course, Rhine knew that many people would be skeptical of such findings and might suspect that his results were due to cheating or even fraud, so over time, he made his experiments increasingly sophisticated and carefully controlled. He also changed from having people guess the next card in a deck of Zener cards to guessing the roll of dice.

- Some of Rhine's studies seemed to show that people could display psychic ability under controlled laboratory conditions. Of course, many people—scientists and nonscientists alike—didn't believe it. Rhine's methods and analyses were carefully critiqued and often criticized, but statisticians came to his defense, arguing that his analyses were valid.

- Since Rhine's ground-breaking work, thousands of studies have investigated a broad array of parapsychological effects. The results have been mixed: Some of these studies have had intriguing success, and some have been obvious failures, so the question is whether the bulk of the evidence supports the existence of psi.

**The Ganzfeld Procedure**

- A special approach to studying ESP is called the ganzfeld procedure. The idea behind using the ganzfeld procedure is that ESP may be so weak that it is often covered up by all of the stimuli coming in through our senses. If so, cutting a person off from normal sights and sounds may make it easier for ESP to operate.

- In the ganzfeld procedure, the participant's goal is to try to pick up what's in another person's mind. While one person—the receiver—relaxes with a covering over his or her eyes and perhaps with headphones emitting a soft hissing noise that covers up any noises in the laboratory, another person sitting in another room— the sender—is shown a randomly chosen picture and told to try to send that image to the receiver mentally for 30 minutes.

- When time is up, the covering and headphones are removed, and the receiver is shown a set of four pictures, one of which is the picture that the sender was trying to send. The receiver is supposed to choose the picture he or she thinks the sender was viewing—the picture that most closely resembles the thoughts and images that were going through the receiver's mind during the study.

- If the receiver is just guessing, he or she has a one in four chance of choosing the picture that the sender was sending, but many of the ganzfeld studies showed that receivers chose the correct picture significantly more often than 25 percent.

- Admittedly, the results of any one experiment, no matter how it turns out, could be affected by all kinds of extraneous factors. That's the case in all research. Fortunately, dozens of ganzfeld studies have been conducted over the years.

- When researchers want to examine the combined findings of many studies that have investigated the same phenomenon, they turn to a statistical procedure called **meta-analysis**, which statistically combines the results of many studies to reach a general conclusion. Although any particular study is subject to all kinds of possible biases and chance findings, combining the results of many studies— conducted by different investigators in different laboratories on different samples—should show us the true, overall effect.

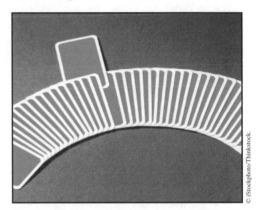

- The first meta-analysis of the ganzfeld studies looked at 28 experiments, and the average hit rate was 35 percent instead of the expected 25 percent. The statistical probability of

**Researchers have tried to discover psychic abilities by having people guess the next card in a sequence of cards.**

participants guessing the right picture 35 percent of the time by chance alone is about one in a billion.

- There are alternative explanations of these findings, however. One thing that could make it seem that participants in the ganzfeld studies selected the right picture at such a high rate is selective reporting. In all scientific fields, studies that obtain significant results are much more likely to be published in scientific journals than studies that don't obtain significant effects, so it's always possible that there are dozens of failed studies that were not reported.

- However, the analyses of statisticians showed that there would have to be an additional 423 fugitive studies that did not find significant effects to cancel out the significant effects of the published studies. Even critics of the ganzfeld research agreed that it's extremely unlikely that there is anything close to that many unpublished ganzfeld studies. Therefore, just about everyone agrees that the positive results of the meta-analysis are not due to selective reporting.

- There could also be methodological problems with the ganzfeld studies that led receivers to guess the right picture without psychic ability being involved. One candidate for such a problem is sensory leakage, which involves any other way that a receiver might be able to tell which of the four pictures was the target picture other than through ESP.

- For example, if the researcher who is testing the receiver at the end of the study knows which target picture the sender was trying to send, he or she could give it away through nonverbal cues, even accidentally.

- Other analyses showed that even if any flawed studies were disregarded from the meta-analysis, the ganzfeld results remain highly statistically significant. In other words, the ganzfeld studies seem to show that receivers do choose the target picture at above chance levels.

- Researchers started using a slightly different procedure, called the autoganzfeld procedure, to eliminate the possibility of sensory leakage and other kinds of experimental contamination. From beginning to end, computers ran the study with almost no involvement by human researchers. In addition, in many studies using the autoganzfeld procedure, the senders watched short video clips rather than looked at photographs.

- After several studies had been conducted using the autoganzfeld procedure, another meta-analysis was conducted that showed an average hit rate across 11 studies of 34 percent; the odds against these results occurring by chance were about 45,000 to one. As with the original ganzfeld studies, receivers seemed to be able to pick up information about the target video clip.

- Much has been written about the ganzfeld debate, and there are strong sentiments on both sides. Some researchers are convinced that the ganzfeld and autoganzfeld studies confirm the existence of ESP, and other researchers just as adamantly deny it.

## Precognition and Presentiment

- **Precognition** involves awareness of some future event, and **presentiment** involves feeling something that has not yet happened.

- In one type of precognition study, research participants are shown a set of objects, and they are asked to guess which object a computer will randomly select in the future. After the participant guesses, a program on the computer randomly chooses one object. The question is whether participants can guess in advance what the computer is going to choose.

- A meta-analysis showed that participants accurately chose the object that would be randomly chosen in the future far above chance levels.

- In presentiment studies, researchers test whether participants have emotional reactions to stimuli that they haven't experienced yet. Participants sit in front of a computer screen and are attached to equipment that measures their level of physiological arousal. Then, a picture appears on the screen for three seconds and then disappears, and this process is continuously repeated.

- Sometimes, the pictures are nature scenes and landscapes that should calm you down, but other times, the pictures are emotionally arousing—pictures of violent scenes or horrible accidents—which should increase your emotional arousal. Seeing the emotional pictures produces a spike in arousal that the calm pictures do not, and people who are going to see an emotional picture begin to show an increase in physiological arousal a few seconds before the picture appears. The likelihood that the presentiment effects obtained in various studies are due to chance is less than one in 125,000.

- When one looks at the research objectively, the ganzfeld studies seem to offer evidence that people can receive images from a person sitting in another room, and the precognition and presentiment studies provide evidence that people can anticipate the future—at least by a few seconds.

- If these research findings involved phenomena that were less strange, they would be strong enough to be accepted by the scientific community without much question. The question for many scientists is whether the evidence thus far is extraordinary enough to support the extraordinary claims. Some scientists think it is; others think it isn't.

## Important Terms

**meta-analysis**: An analysis that statistically combines the results of many studies to reach a general conclusion.

**parapsychology**: The field that studies anomalous psychic experiences such as extra-sensory perception (ESP).

**precognition**: The awareness of some future event.

**presentiment**: The feeling of something that has not yet happened.

**psi**: Psychic phenomena.

## Suggested Reading

Horn, *Unbelievable*.

Krippner and Friedman, eds., *Debating Psychic Experience*.

1. How are the ganzfeld and autoganzfeld procedures used to study ESP, and what does research using these procedures reveal?

2. What is meta-analysis, and how is meta-analysis used to review scientific studies?

# Why Don't Adolescents Behave like Adults?
## Lecture 17

Most people have a somewhat negative impression of what adolescents are like—that they're moody, emotional, and impulsive; that they make bad decisions and take unnecessary risks; and that they overreact to unimportant incidents. However, the emotional volatility that adolescents experience doesn't necessarily indicate that they are inherently different from adults; sometimes, the types of behaviors they display are simply indications that they are dealing with massive life changes. The brain systems that promote mature judgment take time to develop, so there's not much that can be done to help adolescents better self-regulate until their brains are ready.

**Developmental Psychology**

- Experts in **developmental psychology**, the scientific field that studies how people change over the lifespan, view the period of life known as **adolescence** as ranging from about age 12 to about age 19—basically, the teenage years. Adolescence starts with the onset of puberty, which differs across people, and it ends when the person is functioning as an adult, which also varies.

- It wasn't until the start of the 20th century that anything like modern adolescence began to emerge in the United States. Two social changes led to this transitional stage in which people past puberty were not yet considered to be adults. First, child labor and universal education laws were enacted that largely kept teenagers out of the work force and in secondary school longer than they once did. Then, as a greater proportion of high school graduates started going to college, full-fledged adulthood was postponed even further.

- Some of the behaviors that characterize adolescence may reflect living in the world between childhood and adulthood. In cultures in which people reach adulthood earlier, people in the adolescent age range don't show many of the characteristics that we associate with adolescence in this country.

- The idea that adolescents are inherently emotional and conflicted entered modern psychology through G. Stanley Hall, a psychologist who was instrumental in starting the fields of developmental and educational psychology. Hall described adolescence as a time during which young people start contradicting their parents, show volatile swings in their moods, and behave in reckless and antisocial ways.

## Stereotypes of Adolescents
- People's stereotypes of adolescents center on three interrelated patterns of problem behaviors: conflicts with parents and other authority figures, moodiness and strong emotions, and impulsivity and risk taking.

- Research confirms that children's conflicts with their parents increase in early adolescence compared to immediately beforehand—in preadolescence—but the level of conflict typically remains high for only a couple of years before it declines as teenagers move into later adolescence.

- Most of the conflicts that adolescents have with their parents focus on rather minor issues, such as their personal appearance, dating, family rules, and curfews. Studies show that most adolescents tend to agree with their parents on more important issues.

- Much of the conflict between parents and adolescents seems to occur because teenagers are establishing their independence from their parents—which is an essential part of growing up—but their parents are having trouble letting go of a maturing teenager.

- In addition, research evidence shows that adolescents report more rapid and extreme swings in their moods—both positive and negative—than either preadolescents or adults do. Longitudinal studies that follow people yearly through childhood and adolescence show that negative moods increase during the transition from preadolescence to adolescence.

- A popular explanation is that adolescent moodiness is caused by hormonal changes that occur at puberty. When puberty sets in, boys and girls start producing hormones that are responsible not only for changes in their physical bodies, but also changes that are associated with mood.

- Research shows that the concentration of certain hormones is related to the strength of adolescents' moods, and fluctuations in those hormones are related to how much their moods change.

- Mood swings may also be due to cognitive and situational changes that occur when teenagers enter puberty. Adolescents display new mental capabilities for abstract reasoning that allow them to see complexities in life that they couldn't see as a child, and life becomes more complicated and stressful as children turn into teenagers.

- Various changes in adolescents' roles add up to a lot of stress, and people who are under stress are often moody. Adolescence involves major personal and social changes and transitions that would be stressful at any age, but for a young person without much life experience, these changes can be overwhelming.

- Furthermore, in the United States and most other Western countries, people in their teens and early twenties show the highest rates of **risky behaviors**, which have the potential to harm themselves or other people. Adolescents show high rates of alcohol and drug use, risky automobile driving, unsafe sexual behavior, and sometimes criminal actions.

- A popular view is that adolescents take so many risks because they think that they are somehow invulnerable, but research doesn't support the stereotype of adolescents as irrational people who think that they're invulnerable or who are unaware of, or unconcerned about, potential risks in life.

- In fact, most studies don't find notable differences in adolescents' and adults' judgments of how much risk is involved in various behaviors, and adolescents and adults don't differ much in how serious they think the consequences of risky behaviors are.

- Additionally, when we try to reduce risky behavior by giving adolescents additional information about the dangers of taking drugs, driving recklessly, or having

**Despite their conflicts, most adolescents and their parents rate their relationships with each other as fairly good.**

unprotected sex, that information usually doesn't change their behavior, which suggests that the problem doesn't involve their judgments of risk.

### Adolescents and Brain Networks

- Research in neuroscience suggests that adolescents' risk taking may be due to the way in which the brain develops during adolescence; specifically, it might involve the interplay between two distinct networks in the brain.

- The socioemotional network is particularly important for processing information about rewards and, especially, social rewards. This socioemotional network is remodeled neurologically by the hormonal changes of puberty. At the onset of puberty, the reward centers of the brain change so that young people begin to pay more attention to potentially rewarding experiences and events. Therefore, adolescents have different brains than children do.

- This network not only becomes more active, but it also becomes more fully interconnected with other parts of the brain, including areas that are used to process social information. As a result of changes in the socioemotional network, social factors—including social rewards—start to play a more important role in behavior after people enter puberty.

- The cognitive control network is involved in what cognitive psychologists call executive processes, which involve functions such as planning and controlling one's impulses.

- Unlike the socioemotional network, which develops rather quickly at the time of puberty, the cognitive control network matures gradually during adolescence and into young adulthood. Therefore, there's one system that involves reactions to things that entice us because they look fun and exciting, particularly when social rewards are involved, and there's another system that helps us decide whether to do these things and stops us when doing them is not a good idea.

- The mismatch between the early development of the socioemotional system and the later development of the cognitive control system may explain some of the impulsivity and risk taking that we see during adolescence. This discrepancy between the two networks shows up mostly when adolescents' behaviors are being influenced by social and emotional factors.

- Much of the psychological research in this area shows that adolescents and adults don't differ much in how they make decisions about risk. Adolescents mostly take risks when they are with their peers and when something looks fun and rewarding, which may help to explain why so much adolescent risk-taking behavior occurs in groups.

- The competition between the socioemotional network and the cognitive control network may also help to explain peer pressure. Sometimes adolescents' peers actively pressure them to do something they probably shouldn't do, but most of the time, adolescents are choosing to do dangerous things voluntarily because the socioemotional network processes information about rewards and social situations all at once. Having peers around makes risky situations more rewarding because they activate the same brain circuitry.

- Susceptibility to peer influences—including direct peer pressure—increases in early adolescence. Then, it peaks in mid-adolescence and gradually declines into adulthood as the cognitive control network matures.

- Not only does susceptibility to peer pressure change with age, but peers also have a different effect on risk taking among teenagers than among adults. This pattern of changes in reactions to peer influences may occur because of the difference in the rates of development of the socioemotional and cognitive control systems.

- At one time, the socioemotional and cognitive control networks may have developed at closer to the same age in adolescents, but with the age of puberty declining, the socioemotional network may now become active at an earlier age than it once did. As a result, adolescents today have a longer span of time in which the urges and emotions arising from the socioemotional system are not held in check by the cognitive control network.

- Another reason that the socioemotional and reward systems may mature sooner than the cognitive control system is that it's actually beneficial for people moving from childhood to adulthood to be open to novel experiences and to a certain degree of risk. Some scientists even suggest that evolution may have built these characteristics into the adolescent psyche because they are beneficial for development.

- The younger a child is when he or she reaches puberty, the less developed the cognitive control network will be, and the longer the adolescent will have an active socioemotional network without a mature cognitive control network to keep it in check.

## Reducing Risky Behavior

- Research shows that beyond a certain point, simply providing information about the dangers of risky behavior doesn't have much of an effect on adolescents' risky behavior. Whether adults like it or not, adolescents are likely to take risks until the cognitive control system is more fully developed, and there's not much evidence that we can speed up that process.

- Perhaps the best strategy is to monitor and control adolescents' risky behaviors externally. For example, if we more vigilantly enforced laws that govern the sale of alcohol, expanded adolescents' access to contraception and mental health services, and raised the driving age, we would be more effective in limiting adolescent substance abuse, pregnancy, and automobile accidents than trying to make young people make better and less impulsive decisions.

- In thinking about adolescent behavior, we need to be fair. Adults do their share of irrational, impulsive, and inexplicable things, so we shouldn't use adolescence as an explanation for behaviors that are common to people of all ages.

- When we think of adolescent risk taking, we normally think of dangerous kinds of behavior, but risk taking also includes trying new things in school, sports, or social relationships. In fact, research shows that a moderate amount of risk taking and experimentation is associated with a high level of social competence among teenagers.

## Important Terms

**adolescence**: The period ranging from about age 12 to about age 19 that starts with the onset of puberty and ends when the person is functioning as an adult.

**developmental psychology**: The scientific field that studies how people change over the lifespan.

**risky behavior**: A behavior that has the potential to harm oneself or other people.

## Suggested Reading

Steinberg, *You and Your Adolescent.*

Walsh, *Why Do They Act That Way?*

## Questions to Consider

1. Why do adolescents tend to be more moody than adults?

2. Neuroscientists suggest that certain problematic adolescent behaviors occur because of a difference in the rates at which the socioemotional network and the cognitive control network develop. Describe how this developmental difference explains adolescent risk behaviors.

# How Much Do Men and Women Really Differ?
## Lecture 18

A lthough many of the conflicts that arise between men and women are due to the notion that they are inherently different from one another and, therefore, cannot understand each other, men and women are not as different as they assume. Research has shown that even when differences are detected, most of them are quite small. Furthermore, the differences that exist must be viewed against the backdrop of men's and women's similarities as human beings. On average, men and women are far more similar in areas of personality, cognitive ability, sexuality and mating, and psychology than they are different.

**Comparing Men and Women**

- Any given study that compares men and women gives us only a tentative estimate of the size of the difference between men and women for any given attribute because the effects of any particular study depend on the specific sample, measures, and methods used in that study.

- However, if we combine the results of many studies of the same psychological characteristic—verbal ability or self-esteem, for example—we obtain the average, or typical, difference between men and women across all of the studies that have been conducted.

- Meta-analysis provides a more accurate estimate of how much men and women differ on a particular characteristic than the results of any particular study. By conducting a meta-analysis, we obtain a statistical index of the size of a particular difference between men and women—for example, in math ability or in empathy—and this statistic is called the **effect size**.

- For example, a meta-analysis was conducted on 47 studies that measured how far men and women can throw various things, and the average size of the difference across those 47 studies was calculated. This effect size—the size of the difference in throwing distance—was very large, which indicates that men and women greatly differ in how far they can throw things.

- On average, men are stronger and faster than women. Meta-analyses show that effect sizes for grip strength and running speed are medium in size—with men being better in both of these areas. However, women are more flexible on average than men, and this difference is also medium in size.

- Meta-analysis can't tell us anything about whether these differences between men and women are due to inborn physical differences or to social and cultural influences, but the differences are probably due to both. Men do have greater muscle mass than women, but people also tend to socialize young boys to throw baseballs and footballs more than young girls.

## Differences in Personalities

- One of the largest gender differences in personality lies in the fact that women score higher than men on measures of agreeableness, which has to do with the degree to which people are friendly, nice, and cooperative.

- The effect size for the average difference in agreeableness between men and women is pretty large. About half of all men and half of all women are comparable in agreeableness, but there are more men who are low in agreeableness and more women who are high in agreeableness. As a result, the average woman tends to be nicer and more agreeable than the average man.

- On the other hand, men are more aggressive than women on average. Across dozens of studies, men score higher than women on both physical and verbal aggression with medium effect sizes.

- Other than agreeableness and aggressiveness, there aren't many other major personality differences between men and women. On average, men tend to be a little less conscientious, a little less dependable, and a little less responsible than women. Women on average are just a little more emotional than men, but the effect size is smaller than many people might expect. Men and women are about equally happy, and they are equally satisfied with their lives.

- In the past, scientists assumed that most differences between men and women were inborn, but it became increasingly clear that culture, socialization, and learning play a major role in how boys and girls learn to behave. For a while, the assumption was that most sex differences are due to cultural and social factors.

- The problem with this view is that all other mammals show inborn differences in the behaviors of males and females, so it would be very strange if none of the differences between human males and females were due to biological differences.

- In modern times, most scientists believe that men and women differ biologically in ways that influence their behavior, but culture also plays a large role in creating gender differences.

**Differences in Cognitive Abilities**
- Research on gender differences conducted in the 1970s concluded that women were better than men in verbal skills but that men were better than women in math ability. However, meta-analyses show that women's advantage in vocabulary and reading ability is miniscule.

- The data for math is mixed. A meta-analysis of over 40 studies showed that men score slightly above women on math problem solving, but women score slightly higher than men on math computations. Both of these differences are very small.

- One area in which men consistently score higher than women, with medium effect sizes, involves spatial tasks. Men are better at mentally rotating objects in their mind to imagine what they would look like from other angles.

## Differences in Sexuality and Mating

- Studies of attitudes toward sex support the stereotype that men, on average, are more casual about sex than women are, and meta-analyses show that the size of the difference is rather large.

- Generally, women tend to be more careful and less casual than men about selecting sexual partners—which is puzzling because through the generations, reproduction would have been equally important to men and women.

- Evolutionary biologists have suggested that males and females of many species, including human beings, differ in their sexual behavior because of biological differences between the sexes.

- One difference involves reproductive constraint: Women have the potential to have fewer offspring during their lifetime than men do. Women have a limited number of reproductive years and generally have only one child at a time, but a man's potential to father children is almost unlimited.

- Another biological difference between men and women is their parental investment. Among mammals, females of the species invest more in their offspring, biologically speaking, than males do. They have to carry the baby from conception to birth, eat enough during pregnancy to supply it with nutrients, and after the baby's birth, continue to supply enough energy to provide milk. By comparison, a male's biological investment is small; biologically, it costs a man almost nothing to father a child.

- From an evolutionary standpoint, if women can have fewer offspring and must invest more biologically in each child, they have to be more careful not to squander their reproductive opportunities on poor choices of mates. However, because men can potentially father many children, they could afford to be less choosy in who they mated with. In fact, the men who had the most children throughout evolution may have been the least selective.

- As a result of these differences in reproductive constraint and parental investment, women today may be biologically predisposed to be more sexually selective than men are.

- There's also evidence that men and women look for somewhat different things in their mates. Some of these differences may be built in by evolution, and some of them are probably cultural.

- Research shows that certain things are valued by both men and women. In particular, both men and women want their mates to be kind and understanding, and both prefer their partners to be reasonably intelligent and capable.

- In every society, husbands tend to be older than wives. During the course of evolution, successful breeders had to find a mate who was fertile. For women, finding a fertile man was not much of a challenge because men can be fertile for their entire lives. However, men had more of a challenge because women are fertile for only a portion of their lifespan, and they're constrained to a limited number of children.

- Reproductively, men were most successful when they paired with a mate who could produce the largest possible number of children. As a result, men who preferred women who were younger than themselves had a reproductive advantage in terms of how many offspring their mate could potentially have.

- In addition, women's reproductive success would have been facilitated by mating with a slightly older man who had status and power and could provide for their children. Having a mate with these resources would have increased the likelihood that the children would survive to reproductive age and have children of their own.

## Psychological Differences

- Reproductively, men are more dispensable than women. Because one man can father many children, it's possible for a relatively small group of men to father a disproportionate number of children—in which case, all other men are reproductively dispensable. In certain species, including certain human societies, an alpha male does most of the mating, and a large number of low-status males may never mate or have offspring.

- DNA evidence suggests that only about a third of our ancestors were men. Most women reproduced, but not all males did, and many of those who did reproduced at a lower rate than most women. Therefore, evolutionarily, males were more dispensable than women. Most modern cultures insist on monogamy, which will produce a more even balance, but anthropologists and biologists assume that polygamy was common in the past.

© iStockphoto/Thinkstock.

**For many people, one of the recurring challenges of daily life involves dealing with members of the other gender.**

- Because most women were likely to have children, they didn't have to go out of their way to do things to increase their chances. As a result, no special motives or behaviors were needed to promote having babies.

- Men faced a different situation. If only some men would ever mate and have children, men had to take special action to attract a partner. They would have to show that they had something special that would lead a woman to choose them over other men.

- The fact that men were more expendable in the mating game helps to explain why men throughout history have focused on seeking recognition through military exploits, politics, exploration, and similar achievements in ways that most women have not. In other words, evolutionary processes bred men to seek attention and take risks.

- Many hypotheses have been offered for why men have dominated societies throughout history, but perhaps it's because modern men are the descendents of men who outcompeted others. Women don't have this relentless competitive urge to the same degree because it didn't provide any reproductive benefits for them—they were likely to have children no matter what.

- In modern times, all of this masculine showing off isn't particularly useful. In a monogamous society, men and women have about equal chances of having children. Therefore, this is another case of evolved behaviors that were much more valuable in our ancestors' environment than they are today.

### Important Term

**effect size**: A statistical index of the size of a particular difference between the things that are being studied.

## Suggested Reading

Eliot, *Pink Brain, Blue Brain.*

Hyde, "The Gender Similarities Hypothesis."

## Questions to Consider

1. On what psychological characteristics does research show that men and women differ?

2. According to evolutionary theory, why did sex differences in reproductive constraint and parental investment lead to differences in men's and women's approaches to sexuality?

# Why Do We Care What Others Think of Us?
## Lecture 19

Contrary to the idea that a concern with other people's impressions of oneself is superficial, inauthentic, or maladaptive, it's actually a natural, normal, and adaptive human motive to pay attention to one's public image and to selectively present images that help to achieve one's goals. However, in addition to the ethical issues that arise when people convey images of themselves that they know are not true, excessive concerns with other people's impressions can lead to social anxiety and cause people to manage their impressions in ways that are hazardous to their health.

### Impression Management
- Normal human beings are concerned with how they are perceived by others. People who aren't bothered when others view them in undesired ways generally show signs of having psychological problems. Sociopaths, for example, are relatively unconcerned with what other people think of them.

- People are sometimes concerned about other people's impressions when they shouldn't be, and people's efforts to make certain impressions sometimes lead them to do things that they shouldn't. However, the fact that people's image concerns sometimes lead to undesired outcomes doesn't mean that people should never be concerned with what other people think of them. In fact, that would not be beneficial for anyone.

- When people interact with one another, they are interacting with the impressions that they have formed of each other in their minds. Whether their impressions of each other are accurate or inaccurate doesn't matter.

- Because all of our social interactions are mediated by the impressions that we have of each other, people must pay attention to how other people perceive them, and it's sometimes in their best interests to manage their behavior in ways that convey the kinds of impressions they want other people to form.

- Most desirable outcomes in life depend on being perceived in particular ways. For example, to have friendships and romantic relationships, people have to be viewed in ways that show that they have characteristics that make them good friends and partners.

- Our effectiveness in life depends on the impressions that other people form of us. There are relatively few important outcomes in life that are not affected by the impressions that we make.

- People don't form accurate impressions of us automatically. They usually can't pick up much information from just being with us, so we must help them along by being sure that the impressions they are forming are the ones we want them to form.

- Over the past 50 years, researchers in psychology, sociology, and other fields have conducted many studies to understand the ways in which people manage their public impressions and the ways in which their efforts to manage impression influence their behavior.

- Most of the time when people manage their impressions, they aren't conveying impressions of themselves that aren't true—they aren't being inaccurate or inauthentic. Instead, they're selecting the images that will make the impressions they want to make in a particular situation from all of the different true things they could convey about themselves.

- People can't reveal everything there is to know about them in any given interaction, so they choose the tidbits of information that will help them achieve their current goals. If people were completely unconcerned with what others thought of them, they wouldn't tailor the information and images they present about themselves to the particular person they are talking to or the particular situation they are in—but they do.

- Of course, people sometimes exaggerate and even lie about themselves. Social norms and moral values discourage this, of course, but even so, we all engage in self-presentational lies from time to time.

- Some people misrepresent themselves to get what they want much more than most of us do, and the people to really watch out for are those who score high in **Machiavellianism**, which is a personality characteristic that involves doing whatever it takes to get other people to do what you want, including being deceptive and dishonest and presenting images of oneself that are not accurate.

- Machiavellians are unbridled impression managers; they present whatever public image will get them what they want, as long as they think they can get away with it. When researchers examined the degree to which the images that people present to others are consistent with how they actually see themselves, people who score high on the Machiavellianism scale conveyed much more inaccurate impressions of themselves than people who scored low in Machiavellianism.

- Unfortunately, people who approach social interactions with a Machiavellian philosophy are very good at getting other people to do what they want them to do. Because they don't mind projecting false images of themselves and lying in other ways, they can be quite persuasive.

**Making Negative Impressions**

- Most of the time, people prefer to make positive rather than negative impressions on other people. Normally, you want other people to see you as friendly, competent, ethical, and attractive rather than as unfriendly, incompetent, unethical, and ugly. However, there are times when people think that they can achieve their social goals better if other people form unflattering impressions of them.

- People sometimes try to appear incompetent if being seen as uninformed or even inept has benefits for them. For example, people sometimes play dumb—act like they know less than they really do—when they think that appearing less knowledgeable or less competent will make a better impression.

- People also convey images of being less capable than they really are so that other people won't ask them to do things that they don't want to do. For example, some teenagers use this tactic to avoid certain household chores.

- People also convey negative images of being intolerant, impatient, and hostile when it leads other people to do what they want them to do. Many bosses uphold an image of being critical and demanding to their employees. Such negative images won't win a person many friends, but they do keep other people in line.

- There's even evidence that people will foster an impression of being psychologically troubled when seeming to be disturbed has benefits for them. A classic study showed that hospitalized mental patients exhibited significantly fewer symptoms of schizophrenia when it was in their interests to appear mentally healthy than when being seen as mentally ill had benefits for them, in which case they came across as much more psychologically troubled.

## Social Anxiety

- Although monitoring how we're viewed by others is normal, it has a couple of downsides: It causes social anxiety and can lead to dangerous behaviors.

- Just about everybody has experienced **social anxiety**, the nervousness that people feel on job interviews or on dates, when meeting new people, while being at a social gathering where they don't know anybody, or when speaking in front of groups.

- Feelings of social anxiety are directly tied to people's concerns with the impressions that other people are forming of them. People feel nervous in social situations when they are motivated to make some impression on one or more other people but aren't certain that they will successfully make the impression they desire.

- Anything that increases people's desire to make an impression or that lowers their expectation of making the impression they want to make increases feelings of social anxiety. The worst possible situation, then, is to be highly motivated to make a desired impression but to be fairly certain that you won't be able to make it.

- No one likes to experience social anxiety, but like other negative emotions, social anxiety is often useful because it alerts us to situations in which we need to pay special attention to how we're coming across to other people. However, social anxiety can also become a problem when it leads people to avoid social situations or causes them to have trouble interacting successfully.

- When people feel socially anxious, their natural tendency is to become quiet and somewhat inhibited or withdrawn. In fact, if you don't think that you will make the impression that you want to make—or, worse, if you think that you'll make a blatantly undesired impression—it's not a bad idea just to keep quiet. However, being reticent and inhibited can create problems of their own, and people may worry that their quietness and awkwardness will make an even worse impression.

- People who are high in social anxiety can fall into a cycle in which worrying about their impressions causes them to feel anxious, then their anxiety leads them to clam up and hang back from interactions, which then makes them more anxious about the impressions they are making, which leads to even greater anxiety.

- From a social psychological standpoint, monitoring how one is perceived and evaluated by others can be very beneficial, and it's possible that these concerns have an evolutionary basis as well. People who were motivated to control how they were seen by other people probably survived and reproduced at a higher rate than people who didn't care about how others viewed them.

## Dangerous Behaviors

- People are sometimes too concerned with what other people think of them or are too worried about others' impressions when it really doesn't make any difference. Furthermore, in their desire to make impressions on others, people sometimes do things that are harmful to themselves or to others.

- A large number of accidents and injuries are caused by people's deliberate actions, and sometimes the person was doing whatever caused the accident or injury for self-presentational reasons. One of the best examples is when teenagers drive too fast in order to impress their friends.

- This kind of self-presentational behavior is more characteristic of males than females—not necessarily because males are naturally more reckless than females, but because they want to be seen as fearless or cool, and these kinds of images seem to be more valued among males than among females.

- People's concerns with others' impressions of them can even give people cancer. There are at least a million new cases of skin cancer in the United States each year, and a large proportion of those cases are caused by people purposefully trying to be tan. Unfortunately, people judge pictures of people with a tan more favorably than exactly the same picture of the person without a tan.

Every year, thousands of car accidents involve teenage drivers that were speeding to impress their passengers.

- Some people assume that as people get older, they don't

worry about what other people think of them. It's probably true that people are more discriminating in their use of self-presentation as they age, but it's certainly not true that older people don't care what other people think of them.

- One thing that many older people really care about is that they don't want to be perceived as old. An unbelievable amount of money is spent each year on products and services to help people look younger.

- In American culture, older people are not viewed or treated as positively as younger adults. In other cultures in which older people are venerated, looking old may actually be a benefit.

- One area where concerns with looking old can have a downside involves older people who resist using assistance walking because they don't want to look old. However, not using assistance—such as using a cane or wheelchair—when it's needed can lead to dangerous falls.

## Important Terms

**Machiavellianism**: A personality characteristic that involves doing whatever it takes to get other people to do what you want, including being deceptive and dishonest and presenting images of oneself that are not accurate.

**social anxiety**: The nervousness that people feel in social situations—such as on job interviews or on dates, when meeting new people, while being at a social gathering where they don't know anybody, or when speaking in front of groups.

## Suggested Reading

Goffman, *The Presentation of Self in Everyday Life*.

Leary, *Self-Presentation*.

1. Why are people concerned with how they are viewed by others?

2. In what ways can people's concerns with others' impressions of them be hazardous to their health?

# Why Are Prejudice and Conflict So Common?
## Lecture 20

E ven in the most open and democratic societies, a lot of prejudice and discrimination still exists based on race, nationality, ethnicity, religion, gender, sexual orientation, and a variety of other group memberships. Prejudice and conflict between groups arise easily and naturally as a result of how people think about their own and other groups, especially when they are competing for resources. Understanding why divisions between groups develop—and the things that can help bring them together—can help you make sense of the common tendencies for people to be prejudiced and to engage in conflict.

**Categorizing People**

- In the 1970s, many psychologists assumed that extreme cases of prejudice resulted from certain personality variables that were associated with a general tendency to be prejudiced and dogmatic. In particular, a lot of research had been conducted on the authoritarian personality, which involves the tendency to be highly prejudiced.

- British social psychologist Henri Tajfel believed that the first step in prejudice and discrimination is the simple act of distinguishing "us" from "them," so he was particularly interested in the processes by which people categorize themselves and other people into groups.

- People seem to have a natural tendency to put people into categories, and after they put them into categories, they start thinking of everybody in that category as being pretty much the same, and they often begin to hold negative attitudes toward them.

- Just putting people into two different groups—even when they are assigned to groups in a random or meaningless way—is enough to get people to start thinking that their group is better than the other group, and they start behaving in ways that benefit their own group and disadvantage the other.

- People show this **in-group favoritism** even if they don't know the members of the other group and even if they don't expect to interact with them in the future. Just being a member of a group leads people to identify with and prefer their own group, develop negative views of the other group, and favor their own group when dividing up rewards.

- With these minimal group effects as a starting point, researchers have taken a look at what makes prejudice and conflict between groups even worse. **Realistic conflict theory** proposes that discrimination and conflict arise when groups are in competition for some scarce resource. Once two groups start competing against one another—whether for important things or relatively unimportant things—prejudice and negative behaviors intensify.

## Forming Groups

- Belonging to a group can offer many benefits. It gives you people to help you when you need it, and it allows you to cooperate with other people on tasks that would be impossible for one person to do alone. Members of a group can pool their resources so that everyone has more available to them than any one person would. Furthermore, groups provide opportunities for social interaction, companionship, and support.

- However, joining up with other people is always a bit of a risk because being in a group is beneficial only if the other members of the group cooperate and reciprocate. It's very easy to be taken advantage of when other people don't do their share. Therefore, people don't try to forge cooperative relationships with everybody they meet because they don't know whether they can trust them.

- Forming a group allows people to obtain the benefits of cooperative relationships while minimizing the possible costs because most groups enforce rules for how members should treat each other.

- Sometimes, we still get taken advantage of by people in our groups, but it happens less within cohesive groups than if we were working with a group of random people who weren't members of an identifiable group. By joining groups selectively, people can obtain the advantages of cooperating with other people while minimizing the risks of being taken advantage of.

- By defining who is "in" and who is "out" of a particular group, group boundaries tell us who is most likely to be cooperative, helpful, and trustworthy. Usually, we can trust the average member of the groups to which we belong more than we can trust and rely on the members of other groups.

- Of course, many of the people who are not members of our groups are perfectly nice, trustworthy people. However, we don't know which ones are trustworthy, and many people who are not in our groups have no incentive to treat us well—or if they are members of competing groups, they may be motivated to work against us.

- As a result, the safest solution is for people to assume that anybody who's not in their group might not be trustworthy. That single somewhat reasonable tactic for protecting ourselves can lead us to view other groups with suspicion and distrust, which can lead to prejudice and conflict.

- A central feature of the prejudice and conflict that develops between groups involves biases that favor members of one's own group and discriminate against members of other groups. It's useful to think of this as two distinct biases: a bias to favor one's own group, and a bias to be against another group. These two biases often go together—but not necessarily.

- In general, the pattern seems to be that people strongly favor their own group but not necessarily wish harm upon other groups. In-group favoritism affects our behavior more than out-group derogation and antagonism.

- Research shows that groups of people are less cooperative and more competitive than individuals are. Social psychologists call this the **interindividual-intergroup discontinuity effect**.

- Sometimes, people who hate some other racial or ethnic group have personal friends who are members of that group. As individuals, they get along fine, but they are prejudiced against each others' group.

- The interindividual-intergroup discontinuity effect is an impediment to groups getting along. Reasonable, unprejudiced people who can get along with members of the other group as individuals change somehow when they get into their group.

- Researchers who have studied this effect have uncovered a number of reasons for it. The first is that people are naturally more suspicious and afraid of groups than they are of individual people. Therefore, when we get together in a group to talk about problems with another group, we construe the situation as more threatening and antagonistic.

**Under the right conditions, groups in conflict can come together, but then they might collide with other groups.**

- In addition, most of us don't like to think of ourselves as unfair, greedy, competitive, or prejudiced. As a result, we usually try to treat other people with civility and cooperation—even if we don't like them. However, interacting in a group of people encourages a competitive mindset, and once people start working as a group, new norms kick in that urge them to act in ways that benefit the group, which sometimes requires working against other groups.

- Furthermore, we tend to think that members of other groups are more similar to each other than they really are. One consequence of this **out-group homogeneity effect** is that people generalize the behavior of one member of the out-group to other members of the out-group—and to the group as a whole. However, this effect does not occur for one's own group.

### Intensifying Prejudice and Conflict

- Given how little it takes to create prejudice, discrimination, and conflict, it's no wonder that people act so badly when there's something truly important at stake. When groups are in a win-lose, or zero-sum, relationship, all of these effects become stronger.

- Prejudice and conflict also intensify when people feel that their group is disadvantaged relative to other groups. When members of a group think that their situation is worse in comparison to other groups, they experience dissatisfaction and frustration, are more likely to derogate members of other groups, and are more likely to behave aggressively.

- These reactions might be reasonable if the advantaged, successful group did something to hold the other group down, but we see this effect even when the more advantaged group isn't responsible for the inequality between the groups.

- Just feeling less powerful or disadvantaged causes people to show more prejudice. This is why it's so important to minimize political and economic inequalities if we want groups in society to stop fighting with each other.

- Prejudice and conflict don't necessarily require competition for scarce resources; prejudice and discrimination are also fed by the perception that another group doesn't share the values, attitudes, and moral standards of one's own group.

- Prejudices arise not only in response to important outcomes such as conflicts over jobs or land, but also to symbolic threats to things that we value. Other animals will fight when something important is at stake—such as food, territory, mates, and protecting offspring—but human beings are the only species that gets into conflicts over ideas and values.

- Social psychologists suggest that prejudice can provide desirable psychological outcomes for some individuals. For example, prejudice against members of another group can make people feel better about themselves.

- Research shows that people who feel insecure about their own abilities and personal characteristics judge others more harshly. Research also shows that people who have suffered a blow to their self-esteem are more likely to discriminate against others than people who just experienced a boost to their self-esteem. Presumably, feeling superior to other people can help people feel better about themselves.

- People who have the greatest desire to feel good about themselves—either because they are in a low-status social group or because they have suffered a momentary setback—are more likely to put other people down.

## Reducing Prejudice and Conflict
- It seems built into the nature of the human psyche to dislike and distrust other groups, so efforts to break down walls between groups have to counteract people's natural tendency to build and defend those walls.

- Research in the social sciences has shown that simply throwing members of opposing groups together is not usually an effective strategy, but it is possible to structure their contact in ways that reduce prejudice and conflict.

- In the 1950s, Gordon Allport described the conditions under which group contact is most likely to reduce negative feelings between groups. First, the groups must have equal status within the situation in which they will have contact and interact with each other. Second, the situation must provide an opportunity for the groups to cooperate toward some common goal. There also must be opportunities for members of the two groups to become personally acquainted. Finally, some higher authority should support the goal of bringing the groups together and reducing conflict.

- Research has shown that we can reduce prejudice by getting members of diverse groups to develop a shared identity. The idea is that we can change the way people categorize themselves from "us" versus "them" to "we." Studies have shown that once the members of two old groups started reconceptualizing themselves as members of the same group, prejudice and conflict declined.

- Unfortunately, when we bring two groups together in this way by stressing their common identity, members of those two groups will start seeing themselves as one group, but the members of the new unified group may start seeing themselves as different from other groups that maybe they hadn't thought much about before.

## Important Terms

**in-group favoritism**: Rating one's own group much more positively than another group.

**interindividual-intergroup discontinuity effect**: The notion that groups of people are less cooperative and more competitive than individuals are.

**out-group homogeneity effect**: The tendency for people to think that members of groups other than their own are more similar to each other than they really are.

**realistic conflict theory**: A theory that proposes that discrimination and conflict arise when groups are in competition for some scarce resource.

## Suggested Reading

Eberhardt and Fiske, eds., *Confronting Racism.*

Sherif, Harvey, Hood, Sherif, and White, *The Robbers Cave Experiment.*

## Questions to Consider

1. What is the minimal group procedure, and what does it tell us about the causes of prejudice and conflict?

2. What conditions are necessary for reducing prejudice when members of two groups are brought together?

# Why Do People Fall In—and Out of—Love?
## Lecture 21

O n the list of all-time mysteries of human behavior, love can be found at the top. Love has been a preoccupation for people for a very long time. Research suggests that some of the problems that people have in their closest relationships come from their unrealistic expectations about love. With greater knowledge about what causes love, how love changes as relationships develop, and the ways in which people can keep their relationships intact over time, people might be able to manage their closest relationships more intelligently and skillfully.

**Studying Love**
- Recent research has shown that we can understand some things about love using scientific methods, and furthermore, most people are very interested in understanding love. People's close relationships are exceptionally important to their well-being.

- Studying love is complicated by the fact that love is often confused with intense liking, and there is a big difference between loving someone and being in love with someone.

- Many years of psychological research support a basic distinction between two fundamental types of love: companionate love and passionate love. **Companionate love** is a strong state of affection that we feel for people with whom our lives are deeply entwined. People can feel companionate love not only for their romantic partners but also for other family members, children, best friends, or members of a tightly cohesive group—such as a military unit or sports team.

- The kind of love that people fall in and out of is called **passionate love**, or romantic love, and it is the kind of love that is intense and exciting at first and that usually involves sexual desire. There's a longing associated with passionate love.

- We can love many people in a companionate sense at the same time, but it's difficult to experience passionate love with more than a couple of people at once, and it usually involves only one person at a time.

## Love and the Brain

- Being in love is obviously a distinct, powerful psychological state, so we ought to be able to find biological markers of it in the nervous system. Indeed, research has identified particular neurotransmitters and patterns of brain activity that are associated with being in love.

- Many people hold a misconception about how men and women differ when it comes to love. Somehow, we've ended up believing that women are more focused on love then men are, but research shows that this stereotype is not true.

- Research shows that men who are in love show just as much activity in brain regions associated with passionate love as women do. In fact, research shows that men may fall in love more easily than women do and suffer more when close relationships don't work out.

- The area of the brain called the caudate nucleus has receptors for a neurotransmitter called **dopamine**. In the right amounts, dopamine creates feelings of exhilaration, gives people additional energy, focuses their attention, and drives them to seek rewards—all of which sound like the reactions of people who are in love.

- A second neurotransmitter that's involved in passionate love is **phenylethylamine (PEA)**, which is a chemical that is related to amphetamines and whose effects on people's mood and energy are similar to those of various stimulants.

- People who experience passionate love feel energized, upbeat, optimistic, and full of energy. Together, the release of dopamine and PEA may explain why people who have fallen in love feel so good and have a zest for life that they don't usually feel.

- Researchers also suggest that the emotional crash and occasional depression that people feel when a passionate love relationship ends resembles the withdrawal symptoms that people experience when they stop taking amphetamines or other stimulants. It's not just that the person is psychologically upset that an important relationship ended, but it's also that those highly arousing, energizing chemicals are no longer being released, resulting in an emotional crash.

- This chemical dependency on dopamine and PEA may be one thing that separates romantic love from companionate love. We're certainly upset when a friendship ends, but people usually don't go through the same desperate withdrawal that they experience when someone with whom they're passionately in love leaves them.

- Dopamine and PEA seem to fuel energy and passion, but being in love also involves feeling a close psychological connection with the other person, and that aspect of being in love involves **oxytocin**, which is a hormone that promotes a feeling of social connection and of being bonded. Touching, hugging, and sex release oxytocin, which then makes people feel closer and more emotionally attached.

- The effects of oxytocin on people who are in love look similar to the effects of oxytocin on young infants and their parents—particularly their mothers. Parents and their babies find great enjoyment in mere physical contact, and there's a desire to want to see the other person and to be together. Furthermore, just as new lovers spend a lot of time looking into each other's eyes, parents and infants engage in the same sort of prolonged eye contact.

- Adults who are in love also engage in many of the same comforting gestures that parents and children do, such as sitting close together, putting their arm around the other person, holding hands, and hugging. Even their style of talking—whispering and baby talk—sound similar to how adults talk to babies.

- All of this suggests that the same neurobiological attachment system may be involved, with oxytocin creating similar patterns of behavior between people who are in love as between parents and their young children.

## Love as an Obsession

- One thing that people report when they fall in love is that they can't stop thinking about the other person. In fact, it sometimes seems like they're obsessed. Research shows that it actually is an obsession.

- People with an **obsessive-compulsive disorder (OCD)** have uncontrollable thoughts, feelings, and ideas (obsession) that lead them to feel driven to engage in certain behaviors (compulsion). That sounds a lot like passionate love, in which people obsessively think about the other person and have a strong, persistent desire to be with him or her.

- Scientists have long suspected that people with obsessive-compulsive disorder have problems with **serotonin**, an important neurotransmitter that plays a part in the regulation of mood, sleep, learning, and other processes that involve the brain.

- Researchers in Italy found that people who were passionately in love and those who were diagnosed with obsessive-compulsive disorder showed a similar pattern of serotonin. Passionate love is much like a form of OCD. In fact, it's sometimes difficult to tell the difference between passionate love and psychological disorder.

Love is not an intangible thing that can't be studied scientifically; it is a psychological experience like any other.

- Passionate love can dominate the early stages of a close relationship, but studies from around the world suggest that the early passion does not last. The new feeling of falling in love, with the obsessive longing and high energy, slowly fades with time.

## Love and Physiology

- Physiologically, people in a long-term relationship move from a highly emotional, energized, and obsessive state in which the neurotransmitters PEA and dopamine predominate to a state in which oxytocin is central. Therefore, the individuals may remain firmly bonded, but the obsession and emotional exhilaration decline.

- Evolutionary scientists suggest that the rise and fall of passion in a relationship may be functional from a reproductive standpoint. Passionate love might be a trick that nature plays on people to get them to latch on to a mate long enough to start having offspring.

- After the offspring arrive, evolution doesn't really care whether the parents are passionate anymore. Then, the partners need a cool-headed attachment to each other as they work together to raise a family. Therefore, from an evolutionary standpoint, it may be a good thing that the passion and the obsession decline.

- People who understand that these changes in the trajectory of love are normal and natural—and probably built into the brain—shouldn't be as likely to interpret them as an indication that something is wrong with their relationship. It's easy to interpret the decline of energy, obsession, and passion as a problem with the relationship when, in fact, it's probably the natural course of events.

- Research on the physiological underpinnings of love helps to explain where the feelings come from in general, but it doesn't explain why we fall in love with the particular people that we do.

- Some theorists suggest that romantic love is rooted in people's earliest experiences with closeness and intimacy when they were infants. The stimuli that were associated with comfort and closeness as an infant get imprinted in people's brains. Experiences that we had when we were young condition us to have positive associations to certain kinds of people, and those associations make us feel better around certain people than others.

- Emotion and physiological arousal are what push people into passionate love—from just loving a person to being in love with the person. Normally, something about the other person causes him or her to be emotionally arousing to us. However, it's also possible for people to become physiologically aroused by something that has nothing to do with the person, but if they think the other person is causing the arousal, they can start to have special feelings of attraction for him or her.

- These extraneous sources of emotional arousal won't cause us to suddenly become attracted to just anybody, but if we already think someone is appealing, then arousal—from whatever the source, including watching a scary movie or physically exercising—can provide the additional ingredient to cause people to fall in love. This effect is called excitation transfer.

- Excitation transfer can work in the opposite direction as well. If you mistakenly attribute your arousal from some unrelated source to someone you don't like, you'll like them even less.

- The excitation transfer effect may explain some interesting experiences, including the passionate way in which some couples make up after they fight. One explanation of this phenomenon is that the couple's original argument got them all physiologically churned up, but once they settled their dispute, some of that arousal was still present, and they misattributed their arousal to passionate attraction rather than to anger.

## Love and Culture
- Anthropologists used to think that romantic love was exclusively an invention of Western cultures, but that view has been largely discredited. Scientists now believe that passionate love is part of

human nature that evolved to maintain connections between people for purposes of mating.

- Even though passionate love is an aspect of human nature, its expression is certainly molded by culture. People everywhere experience passionate love, but how people who are in love are expected to behave differs across cultures.

- For example, when people from around the world were asked whether they would marry someone who was otherwise desirable but for whom they felt no passionate love, less than five percent of Americans said they would marry such a person. However, around 50 percent of the respondents from India and Pakistan said that they would marry someone for whom they did not feel passionate love. Of course, those are two cultures in which arranged marriages are still common.

## Important Terms

**companionate love**: A strong state of affection that people feel for others with whom their lives are deeply entwined.

**dopamine**: A neurotransmitter that creates feelings of exhilaration, gives people additional energy, focuses their attention, and drives them to seek rewards.

**obsessive-compulsive disorder (OCD)**: A psychological disorder that involves the existence of uncontrollable thoughts, feelings, and ideas (obsession) that lead people to feel driven to engage in certain behaviors (compulsion).

**oxytocin**: A hormone that promotes a feeling of social connection and of being bonded.

**passionate love**: The kind of love that is intense and exciting at first and that usually involves sexual desire.

**phenylethylamine (PEA)**: A neurotransmitter that is related to amphetamines and whose effects on people's mood and energy are similar to those of various stimulants.

**serotonin**: A neurotransmitter that plays a part in the regulation of mood, sleep, learning, and other processes that involve the brain.

## Suggested Reading

Fisher, *Why We Love.*

Reis and Aron, "Love."

## Questions to Consider

1.  What roles do dopamine, phenylethylamine (PEA), and oxytocin play in passionate love?

2.  What is excitation transfer, and how can it cause people to fall in love—at least temporarily?

# What Makes Relationships Succeed or Fail?
## Lecture 22

**M**ost adults say that their relationships with their partners are a centrally important part of their lives, and of course, people would prefer that their close relationships go well rather than badly. The success of people's relationships depends in part on the people's personalities—both their individual personalities and the ways that the two people's personality styles mesh with each other—but it also depends on the features of the relationship itself. In this lecture, you're going to discover what behavioral research has revealed about successful and unsuccessful relationships.

**Successful versus Unsuccessful Relationships**

- Relationship science is a relatively new field, but we already know a lot about what leads to satisfying and unsatisfying relationships. Much of the research has focused on marriages, but most of what we have learned applies to other kinds of close relationships as well—including cohabiting partnerships and dating relationships— and it applies to both heterosexual and homosexual relationships.

- All relationships are unique, and the things that make a relationship successful and satisfying versus unsuccessful and unsatisfying differ greatly across people, but there are some general patterns. The determinants of relationship success can be broken into two large categories: characteristics of the people and features of the relationship itself.

- Some people have better, happier, and more satisfying relationships because they are simply better relationship partners than other people are. By nature, if a person is disagreeable, hostile, suspicious, or selfish, then that person is likely to have less satisfying relationships than a person who is agreeable, easygoing, trusting, and giving. Research shows that we can predict some of the success of people's relationships by simply measuring certain aspects of their personalities—even before the relationship starts.

- Neuroticism, which involves the degree to which people tend to experience negative emotions such as anxiety and anger, plays a particularly important role in relationship success and satisfaction. People who score high in neuroticism not only tend to experience more bad moods, but their personal unhappiness leads to more unpleasant and negative interactions with other people, including their relationship partners.

- Other research shows that some problems arise in relationships not because either partner's personality creates problems by itself, but because the two people's characteristics don't mesh very well.

- Many people believe that opposites attract, but research shows that when it comes to relationships, it's almost never true. Of course, people don't want their partners to be just like them, but being different is not the same as being opposite. True opposites rarely get along very well.

- One of the few examples where opposites sometimes do get along involves dominant and submissive people. The dominant person likes being in charge, and the submissive person appreciates somebody else taking the lead.

## Interdependence Theory

- When people think about a relationship not working out, they usually think about things that cause people to break up or to get a divorce, but merely staying together is a rather narrow view of relationship success. Therefore, to understand why some relationships work better than others, we need to distinguish between being satisfied or dissatisfied with one's relationship and whether people decide to stay or to leave.

- Research shows that the processes that contribute to satisfaction are not the same processes that lead people to stay in a relationship.

- All relationships bring a combination of rewards and costs of various kinds. If we subtract people's costs in a relationship from the rewards that they receive, we can get an index of their overall outcome from the relationship. A person who has more rewards than costs has a profit from the relationship, and a person who has more costs than rewards is showing a loss.

- Originally, researchers assumed that people who had a profit would be satisfied with their relationship, but that turns out not to be the case.

- According to **interdependence theory**, each of us has a criterion—a standard—for judging whether we are making enough of a profit in our relationships with other people. This criterion is called our **comparison level**, and it's the minimum value of the outcomes that we think we deserve from a relationship. The comparison level is the standard we use to judge our relationship outcomes.

- When our outcome exceeds our comparison level, we're getting more than the minimum payoff we expect from the relationship, and we're satisfied. Additionally, the more our outcome exceeds our comparison level, the more satisfied we'll be. However, when our outcome falls below our comparison level, we're dissatisfied, and we'll be dissatisfied even if our rewards from the relationship exceed our costs and we're making a profit.

- People can be unhappy in a relationship that from an outsider's perspective would appear to be rewarding because their positive outcomes fall below their comparison level. They're not making as much of a profit as they'd like.

- People's standards for judging their outcomes in relationships are based primarily on their previous relationships. People with a history of highly rewarding relationships tend to have higher comparison levels than people who have had a history of troubled relationships.

- Polls indicate that people say that they have more relationship problems and conflicts than people reported in the past. Perhaps this is because people today expect more out of their relationships—their comparison levels are higher.

- Research suggests that people who begin married life with the highest expectations of how wonderful it's going to be are often the least satisfied and fulfilled a few years later because their comparison levels were too high from the beginning—they expected too much.

- People's satisfaction with relationships is due to whether their outcomes exceed their personal comparison level, but whether people stay in a relationship or decide to leave depends on more than whether they are satisfied.

- According to interdependence theory, whether people stay in a relationship depends on their **comparison level for alternatives**, which is the lowest level of outcome that people think that they can get by leaving their current relationship and moving to the best alternative situation—whether that is another partner or simply being out of a relationship altogether.

- In a happy, stable relationship, people's outcomes from the relationship exceed both their comparison level—which makes them satisfied—and their comparison level for alternatives, which keeps them committed to the relationship. They're satisfied and don't think that they can do better elsewhere.

- In a relationship in which a person's outcomes fall below his or her comparison level but above his or her comparison level for alternatives, the person is not happy or satisfied because the outcomes are lower than the comparison level, but the person will stay in the relationship because the comparison level for alternatives is even lower.

- Even more puzzling than people staying in unhappy relationships are cases in which people leave happy ones. From the perspective of interdependence theory, such situations occur when people's outcomes in a relationship fall above their comparison level but below their comparison level for alternatives.

## Relationship Rewards and Costs

- Fundamentally, relationships that work well are those in which people get sufficient rewards, relative to their costs, so that their outcomes fall safely above both their comparison level and their comparison level for alternatives.

- In their efforts to understand why certain relationships work better than others, researchers sometimes study new relationships from the very beginning, recontacting the same couples every so often in an attempt to understand what features of relationships foreshadow later problems.

- In all developing relationships, the perceived costs increase as the relationship grows. At the beginning of any relationship, people are focused mainly on its rewarding aspects, but then they slowly start to see the costs. At this point in any emerging relationship, the realization that the new relationship has some downsides and personal costs creates a lull, or a plateau, in people's satisfaction.

- In successful relationships, the rewards continue to increase, people adjust to the costs, and satisfaction climbs again. However, in unsuccessful relationships, after the usual plateau in satisfaction, rewards don't increase. Therefore, people become dissatisfied and the relationship ends—although it may take awhile for the individuals to realize that it's not going to improve.

- Studies show that the problems that eventually lead people to break up—even after 10 or 20 years—were typically there from the beginning of the relationship. The people were complaining about those things even before they decided to get married.

- Furthermore, satisfaction with marriage generally declines over time, starting in the second year of marriage, on average. One reason for the decline is that people don't put nearly as much effort into being considerate, responsive, and rewarding partners as time goes by. People's declining motivation to make their partner happy can contribute to lower satisfaction—not only for the partner, but ultimately for them as well.

- All of this suggests that the most important thing that makes relationships work is to be a rewarding partner. Furthermore, research is converging on the idea that one key to relationship success involves responsiveness.

- Studies show that one of the best predictors of relationship satisfaction and success is whether the individuals perceive that their

Studies show that the concerns that cause couples to break up don't just appear—they often existed from the beginning.

partner is sufficiently responsive to their needs and desires. The bottom line of responsiveness is whether each partner actively supports and promotes the other person's personal welfare.

- Responsiveness is important because it is very rewarding. As a result, a responsive, supportive partner increases the partner's positive outcomes—hopefully above his or her comparison level and comparison level for alternatives.

- To some extent, responsiveness is in the eye of the beholder. A person might work very hard to be responsive to a partner's needs, but if the person isn't actually doing very helpful things, or if the partner doesn't interpret the person's actions as responsive, then the partner won't view the person as sufficiently responsive.

- People miss a lot of support that their partners give, and they interpret things as supportive that their partners do not intend as such. There's misperception in both directions.

- When people begin to perceive that their partner is not being responsive, they naturally pull back their own efforts to be responsive. Not only does a concern with equity set in, but people also don't want to be hurt by investing more in the relationship than the partner does. Studies that track people's relationship behaviors over time show that this can become a vicious cycle.

- Fortunately, relationship scientists are uncovering the ingredients of successful relationships, and they come down to a few basic things. People who are satisfied with their close relationships feel that they are getting sufficient rewards from the relationship. They are also highly responsive to the needs of their partner and allow themselves to depend on the other person, knowing that the relationship will work only if both people feel understood and cared for.

- Perhaps most importantly, they resist the natural tendency to fall into lazy patterns of disinterest in which they no longer display the rewarding, desirable patterns of behavior that attracted their partner to them in the first place.

## Important Terms

**comparison level**: The minimum value of the outcomes that people think they deserve from a relationship.

**comparison level for alternatives**: The lowest level of outcome that people think that they can get by leaving their current relationship and moving to the best alternative situation—whether that is another partner or simply being out of a relationship altogether.

**interdependence theory**: The relationship theory that states that each of us has a standard, called our comparison level, for judging whether we are making enough of a profit in our relationships with other people.

## Suggested Reading

Harvey and Weber, *Odyssey of the Heart*.

Miller, *Intimate Relationships.*

## Questions to Consider

1. How is the success of people's relationships affected by their own and their partner's personalities?

2. What is responsiveness, and what role does responsiveness play in successful relationships?

# Why Do People Blush?
## Lecture 23

People often blush when they do something that conveys an undesired impression of themselves to other people or when they are observed doing something immoral or socially inappropriate. However, being singled out for positive attention also makes many people blush; people blush when they are complimented, praised, or honored. In general, blushing can be caused by making a bad impression, making a good impression, being stared at, or even being accused of blushing. In this lecture, you will discover why people blush and why certain people blush more often than others.

### Physiology and Blushing

- Physiologically, when people blush, the blood vessels in the face, ears, neck, and upper chest dilate, or expand, and the wider vessels allow more blood to pass through. Therefore, the face heats up from the increased blood flow, and other people can often see the person's face change color.

- Blushing is almost always accompanied by reduced eye contact. When people blush, they avert their gaze—they look away from other people. Sometimes, they just look away or cast their eyes down, but sometimes they actually drop their head. This urge to avert one's gaze is very powerful.

- In addition to reducing their eye contact, people who are blushing often display a nervous, silly smile—not always, but very often. This is strange because when people are blushing, they usually aren't happy and probably don't really feel like smiling, but they do anyway.

- Sometimes people may smile to try to hide how distressed they are. If people play a trick on you and you are embarrassed, you might try to show everybody that you're a good sport by smiling.

- There's no shortage of ways to embarrass, humiliate, and degrade ourselves, and when we do things that damage our image or reputation, we often blush. Because of this, some scientists have concluded that blushing is a response to situations that damage a person's public image. That's often true, but people also blush when very positive events occur and when others seem to think very highly of them.

- In fact, people don't have to have anything in particular that affects their public image at all. Sometimes, people blush when they are just speaking to other people, talking to a group, or being the center of attention. It's very easy to get most people to blush just by having a group of people stare at them.

- Among many species, including human beings, staring is a very powerful social stimulus. Stares are often threatening, so it's interesting that staring alone can cause blushing. Another thing that will cause people to blush is simply being accused of blushing.

## Theories of Blushing

- Charles Darwin was one of the first scientists to write about blushing. Darwin was very interested in emotions and particularly in how emotions evolved. He explored the adaptive functions of various emotions and the ways in which animals, including human beings, express their emotions, but he was extremely puzzled about blushing.

- Darwin recognized that blushing has something to do with people's concerns with how they are viewed by other people, but he didn't think that blushing actually served a purpose.

- Darwin thought that when people focus on a particular part of their body, their self-attention interferes with the contraction of the blood vessels of that body part and makes the vessels dilate. He said that blushing occurs in the face because when we're interacting with other people, they tend to look at our face, which leads us to focus on our own face, leading to a dilation of the blood vessels in the face. However, this reasoning is incorrect.

- Several psychoanalysts have suggested that blushing occurs from repressed exhibitionism. According to this explanation, a person has the unconscious desire to expose himself or herself to other people, but social norms don't allow people to do that. To satisfy that unconscious urge, blood gets channeled from the genitals to the face. However, there isn't any scientific evidence to support this explanation.

- There are two competing explanations that focus on the role of blushing in social interactions. According to the remedial perspective, blushing is a nonverbal signal or acknowledgement to other people that we know that we have broken some rule or violated some norm and that we are sorry about it. In addition, blushing conveys this message quickly and automatically in a way that can't be easily faked. Other people appear to interpret our blushing and other signs of embarrassment as if they are an apology.

- Many people try to hide their blushing from others, but if you have obviously done something incompetent or inappropriate, it's usually better to let other people know that you are embarrassed because they will be much more forgiving if they see you blush.

- The remedial explanation of blushing might not tell the whole story. People

**People who are blushing often display a nervous, silly smile— perhaps to hide how distressed they are.**

sometimes blush even when they haven't done anything wrong or embarrassing—and even when other people are evaluating them positively, as when they are complimented or honored.

- Blushing can be caused by making a bad impression, making a good impression, being accused of blushing, or just being stared at. All of these situations involve undesired social attention. The undesired social attention explanation says that people blush when they receive undesired attention from other people—regardless of whether the attention is positive, negative, or even neutral. This view states that the function of blushing is to get people to stop paying attention.

- Much of the time, we want social attention. We want people to pay attention to us, look at us, listen to us, and interact with us; sometimes, we even feel bad if we're ignored.

- However, sometimes we don't want attention from other people. For example, if we think other people are forming undesired impressions of us, we don't really want them to focus attention on us. This is particularly true if we have made a fool out of ourselves or have been seen doing something bad. In those cases, we don't want attention from other people.

- Sometimes, even positive social attention can be undesired. Of course, we want people to like us and evaluate us positively, but when they single us out for honors or compliments, their attention and scrutiny might be too intense. Being observed closely by many people can make us feel self-conscious, awkward, and uncomfortable—even when all the attention is in our honor.

- When someone else is blushing, you usually look away, change the subject, and divert your attention somewhere else. It usually makes people uncomfortable to look at someone who is blushing. Therefore, blushing shifts the focus of attention away from the person.

## Blushing in Other Species

- One of the provocative things about the behaviors that accompany blushing is that in some ways, they resemble the nonverbal appeasement displays that we see in other apes, including chimpanzees. Many species have **appeasement displays**, which are behaviors that reduce social threats from other members of the species.

- When another member of the species—usually a higher-status one—seems threatening, animals often engage in behaviors that may appease or mollify the threatening animal. If the appeasement display is successful, the threatening animal loses interest and goes away. If it's not successful, the threatening animal may attack.

- Chimpanzees have an appeasement display that bears some similarities to blushing in human beings. Chimpanzees don't appear to blush, but when chimpanzees appease, they do two things than human beings do when we blush.

- First, chimpanzees avert their eyes because looking directly into the eyes of another chimpanzee is often taken as a challenge. In the same way, people invariably avert their gaze and look away when they blush.

- Furthermore, when chimpanzees engage in appeasement display, they often smile a vacant, mirthless grin that looks similar to the nervous, embarrassed, sheepish grin of people when they blush.

- One of main things that causes appeasement displays in chimpanzees is attention from a more dominant animal—particularly when the dominant animal stares at the less dominant one. Similarly, staring can cause people to blush.

- Zoologists, ethologists, and other scientists who study animal behavior have stressed the appeasing functions of these behaviors in chimpanzees and other apes. They're called appeasement displays because they lower the likelihood of aggression. However, the most immediate thing that happens when an animal appeases is that the threatening animal loses interest. Therefore, these displays seem to arise from undesired attention, and they seem to lower undesired attention—just like blushing does.

- Viewed in this way, blushing is something like a human appeasement display. The big question is why we blush when we appease and other animals don't, and scientists don't have an answer to that question.

## The Creeping Blush

- The classic blush arises very rapidly in response to a specific event and then fades pretty quickly, but there is a somewhat different type of blushing that has received much less attention: the creeping blush, which has a much slower onset than the classic blush.

- Unlike the classic blush, which usually starts on the face or ears, the creeping blush starts on the upper chest, becomes splotchy on the neck, and then creeps up to the face and ears. However, even when fully developed, the creeping blush usually has a blotchy appearance. Some people who experience this reaction think that they're developing hives or a rash from being socially anxious, but it's actually a creeping blush.

- Just like the classic blush, the creeping blush seems to be caused by undesired social attention. Most people who show a creeping blush while giving a speech in front of a crowd would probably rather not be speaking in front of the group. Unlike the classic blush, once the person sits down, the creeping blush dissipates very slowly, and evidence of the blush can remain for quite a while.

## Individual Differences

- Some people rarely blush whereas other people blush a lot, and all that blushing creates difficulties for many people because they're embarrassed by how much they blush. Some people blush because they blush too much, so they try to avoid situations in which they might blush.

- If blushing is fundamentally caused by undesired social attention, then the reason that some people blush more than others is that they are more bothered by being the focus of other people's attention. Some people find social attention more troubling—and more undesired—than other people do.

- Some people think more about how they are viewed by other people than other people do. Researchers call this characteristic **public self-consciousness**. People who are high in public self-consciousness are more aware of being the focus of others' attention than people who are low in public self-consciousness.

- In addition, people who are more worried about being evaluated negatively by other people—those who are high in fear of negative evaluation—find social attention more undesired because whenever you are the focus of attention, there's always a possibility that others will evaluate you negatively.

- Furthermore, people who are lower in self-confidence dislike social attention more because they aren't sure that they can handle social situations well.

## Important Terms

**appeasement display**: A behavior that reduces social threats from other members of one's species.

**public self-consciousness**: A characteristic that describes the degree to which a person thinks about how he or she is viewed by other people.

## Suggested Reading

Leary, Britt, Cutlip, and Templeton, "Social Blushing."

Miller, *Embarrassment*.

1. What appears to be the cause of all instances of blushing?

2. In what ways do people's behaviors when they blush resemble the appeasement behaviors of certain nonhuman primates?

# A Few Mysteries We Can't Explain Yet
## Lecture 24

In this lecture series, you've learned about human behavior and about the ways that behavioral researchers tackle difficult questions about why we think, feel, and behave the way we do. As a result, you have probably begun looking at your own and other people's behavior with curiosity and even wonderment. For many of the topics that this course has addressed, at least some of the mystery has been solved. For others, however, researchers have made progress toward understanding certain intriguing phenomena—such as laughing, kissing, creating and enjoying art, and experiencing consciousness—but these behaviors are unusually difficult to explain.

### Unsolved Mysteries of Human Behavior

#### Laughing
- Most people think of laughter as an involuntary physiological response to humor, but it is not necessarily involuntary. Not only do we not laugh at everything that we think is funny—sometimes we just smile or feel amused—but we also laugh at things that are decidedly not funny, such as awkward, dangerous, or tragic things.

- We don't know exactly why people laugh. For more than a hundred years, scientists have suggested several explanations, many of which seem plausible, but none of them is entirely satisfactory.

- For example, some theorists have suggested that laughter is fundamentally about releasing stress, and others have offered the related idea that laughter may reflect an expression of relief after some danger has passed. Likewise, laughter certainly helps people cope with stress and other negative emotions.

- One important clue in trying to understand laughter is the fact that laughter almost always occurs in encounters with other people—

either when other people are actually present or sometimes when we're talking with other people on the phone.

- Even humorous events are much more likely to make people laugh when they're with other people. Something that might merely amuse you when you are by yourself might make you laugh out loud if other people are there. This observation suggests that laughter may be a social signal of some kind—rather than just an expression of emotion or a release of tension.

**Laughter is so normal and natural that you may have never thought about how strange it actually is.**

- However, laughter is not just a signal that you think that an event or another person is funny. Research shows that people who are engaged in a conversation are much more likely to laugh after they say something themselves than they are to laugh at what other people say.

- We usually don't laugh—at least genuinely—around people we dislike. Furthermore, research shows that laughing together brings people closer and improves social relationships. Therefore, maybe laughter is a signal that indicates a desire for social connections.

- Some researchers have suggested that laughter evolved from the play signals that are used by nonhuman primates. Other apes sometimes hoot and holler when they play with each other, and similar behaviors are seen in small children.

- If laughter is a social signal that conveys closeness or connection, then it shouldn't matter what we laugh at—but some things are funnier than others. At present, we have many miniature theories of laughter, but no single theory that covers all instances in which people laugh.

**Kissing**
- Kissing between romantic or sexual partners occurs in about 90 percent of human cultures, and even in cultures where mouth-to-mouth kissing is not accepted, partners often lick, suck, or rub their partner's faces.

- Certain other species kiss, too. Bonobos—one of our closest animal relatives—not only kiss a lot, but they also engage in deep tongue kissing, or so-called French kissing.

- The origins of human kissing may lie deep in our animal past. One theory is that kissing evolved from the behavior of primate mothers passing along chewed-up food to their toothless babies. This might explain why people kiss their children—although not usually on the mouth—but it does not explain how this behavior evolved into an intimate, sensual behavior.

- Another explanation is that kissing evolved as a way of assessing things about a potential partner. Other animals—such as dogs, for example—size each other up by sniffing each other. Human beings don't have the same acute sense of smell that most other mammals do, so maybe we require very close physical contact to provide us with information about another person.

- Research shows that the smell of another person's breath and the taste of someone's saliva can provide information about the person's state of health. There's also evidence that men can detect whether a woman is ovulating through taste and smell. It might also be that people assess the other person's degree of interest and involvement in a relationship by how they kiss.

- Of course, people are not purposefully assessing each other in these ways when they kiss, but it's certainly possible that kissing evolved to put people into contact with the skin and saliva of potential partners to assess certain things about them.

- A third explanation is that, like laughter, kissing promotes social bonding. People report that kissing often increases a sense of closeness, and research studies show that kissing releases hormones—such as oxytocin, which increases feelings of social connection.

- Perhaps that's why not only human beings, but also chimpanzees and bonobos, kiss each other to make up after conflicts and fights, which also supports the social bonding hypothesis.

- A fourth perspective suggests that because kissing can be arousing, it increases sexual interest. The question, though, is whether people kiss mostly to increase their own arousal or to increase the arousal of another person. Regardless, neither explanation answers the question of why contact with the lips, specifically, is involved.

## Creating and Enjoying Art
- Art is all around us. People paint, draw, sculpt, dance, write, perform music and plays, and engage in many other creative and expressive endeavors. People enjoy doing artistic things, and they also enjoy looking at, watching, and experiencing art, but nobody really knows why.

- If behavioral science has taught us anything in the past hundred years it's that when just about every human being in every culture does something, the behavior must either serve some important function today, or it promoted survival and reproduction in the evolutionary past—or sometimes both.

- However, if we're dispassionate about it, art seems an unusual use of people's time. It doesn't seem to be serving any basic survival needs, and it's not obvious what people gain from art that justifies the time, effort, and money that they put into it.

- In the scientific literature, it has been discussed that art serves important social functions. Although there are exceptions, most forms of art either occur in groups—such as singing or dancing—or is done for other people, as when visual artists display their work or when performers sing, dance, or play music for an audience.

- From the standpoint of the painter, musician, dancer, or playwright, art potentially provides social connections to other people—either connections to other painters, musicians, dancers, or playwrights or connections to people who come to view the art. There are a few people who engage in some artistic activity by themselves and never let anybody else know about it, but that's pretty rare.

- Additionally, the enjoyment of art usually occurs in groups. People often go to museums, showings, concerts, and other performances with other people, and art becomes a topic for conversation and for social identification.

- In addition to the social function of art, there is an important expressive aspect to art as well. Artists often talk about using their art to express themselves. People want to express themselves—to let other people know who they are, what they think, and what they are feeling—but it's not clear why people often choose to express themselves in symbolic rather than straightforward ways.

- It's also possible that people often engage in artistic activities more to experience the process than to produce a particular outcome or product. The creation of art often involves a **flow experience**, a psychological state that sometimes occurs when people are fully immersed in an activity.

- When people are in flow, they are so absorbed in what they are doing that they basically lose consciousness of themselves. Flow is an exceptionally pleasurable experience, so some people may create art because it allows them to enter a state of flow. Likewise, some people may experience the pleasure of flow while experiencing art.

- It is very difficult to study spontaneous artistic activity under the kinds of controlled laboratory conditions that would allow us to dissect the experience of art and identify what causes it. Once people know that they are in a research study, the normal psychological processes that underlie their artistic behaviors usually vanish; they're no longer motivated to engage in artistic behaviors for the same reasons that they do in everyday life.

## Experiencing Consciousness

- At the most simple level, the question of consciousness involves what causes sentient animals to be consciously aware of their experiences. There doesn't seem to be much doubt that the brain is involved in consciousness. Obviously, activity in the brain is associated with seeing, hearing, smelling, sensing, and thinking, and if we damage the brain in certain ways, people are no longer conscious.

- Most scientists would agree that the brain is somehow involved in consciousness, but the problem is that nobody has even the slightest idea of how the brain produces consciousness—if it even does.

- Your brain is composed of about 100 billion neurons that send electrical and chemical signals among themselves and that receive input from receptors of various kinds located around the body, such as the receptors in your eyes, ears, or skin. Neurons transmit information, and scientists know a lot about how neurons communicate with each other.

- However, transmitting information is not consciousness. Sentient animals not only receive and process information—about colors, sounds, and physical touch, for example—but they also experience those things consciously.

- Consciousness theorists call the giant chasm between explaining how the brain works and explaining what produces consciousness the **explanatory gap**. We know a lot about how the brain processes information but virtually nothing about how it produces consciousness—despite centuries of philosophy and scientific research.

- Of course, there are many things that scientists don't understand, but consciousness differs from many mysteries in that not only do we not have any viable explanations about where consciousness comes from, but we don't even have an idea about what kind of explanation would make any sense.

- Many of the more recent explanations of how the brain is related to consciousness have tied in ideas from quantum physics. For example, one theory links consciousness to the processes through which the brain integrates information coming from various senses and binds them together into one experience. However, this still doesn't explain why people have conscious experiences.

- The difficulty in making inroads into the question of consciousness has led many scientists and philosophers to suggest that we must be thinking about the question entirely wrong—that our basic assumptions about how the brain works must be somehow incorrect.

- Some experts in consciousness have suggested that we have been wrong in assuming that the brain creates consciousness. Instead, they suggest that consciousness exists outside of us in the external world—like gravity or electromagnetism—and our brains are tapping into and using consciousness rather than creating it.

- Other scientists are convinced that consciousness is an unusually complex process that we simply don't understand yet, but we will someday when we conduct enough research and have more information.

**explanatory gap**: The giant chasm between explaining how the brain works and explaining what produces consciousness.

**flow experience**: A psychological state that sometimes occurs when people are fully immersed in an activity.

## Suggested Reading

Blackmore, *Consciousness*.

Lilienfeld, Lynn, Ruscio, and Beyerstein, *50 Great Myths of Popular Psychology*.

## Questions to Consider

1. In what ways might laughter promote social bonding? Why does the social bonding hypothesis fail fully to explain the phenomenon of laughter?

2. Why do many scientists consider consciousness to be the greatest remaining psychological mystery?

# Glossary

**action tendency**: An impulse to respond in a particular way as a result of a specific emotion.

**activation-synthesis theory**: The first modern theory of dreams that suggests that dreams are the brain's efforts to make sense out of meaningless patterns of firing in the brain while sleeping.

**acute stress**: The type of stress that occurs when people experience an immediate threat to their well-being.

**adolescence**: The period ranging from about age 12 to about age 19 that starts with the onset of puberty and ends when the person is functioning as an adult.

**affective forecasting**: The act of predicting how events will influence one's emotions in the long run.

**akratic action**: The undesired behavior that people sometimes engage in while they are telling themselves that they shouldn't be engaging in the behavior; comes from a Greek word that means a failure of will or self-control.

**allele**: A different form of a gene.

**appeasement display**: A behavior that reduces social threats from other members of one's species.

**behavioral genetics**: The scientific field that studies both the genetic and environmental influences on such characteristics as personality.

**behaviorism**: A branch of psychology that claims that all behaviors and emotional responses are the result of learning.

**catastrophizing:** A thinking process in which a person has an exaggerated view of the likelihood that something bad is going to happen or an exaggerated belief about how bad the bad thing is.

**catharsis**: The act of purging one's emotions.

**chronic stress**: The type of stress that almost always exists.

**cognitive appraisal theory**: A theory that claims that each specific emotion is elicited by a particular kind of cognitive appraisal, which is the person's assessment of the impact of the event on his or her well-being and personal concerns.

**cognitive psychologist**: A scientist who studies thinking and memory.

**companionate love**: A strong state of affection that people feel for others with whom their lives are deeply entwined.

**comparison level**: The minimum value of the outcomes that people think they deserve from a relationship.

**comparison level for alternatives**: The lowest level of outcome that people think that they can get by leaving their current relationship and moving to the best alternative situation—whether that is another partner or simply being out of a relationship altogether.

**consolidation theory**: A theory of dreams that suggests that dreams are involved in the storage of memories from the previous day.

**culture**: All of the socially transmitted beliefs and behavior patterns in a group or society.

**delayed-return environment**: An environment in which people invest a great deal of time and effort each day into tasks that don't have any immediate rewards, without knowing whether their efforts will pay off in the future.

**developmental psychology**: The scientific field that studies how people change over the lifespan.

**dopamine**: A neurotransmitter that creates feelings of exhilaration, gives people additional energy, focuses their attention, and drives them to seek rewards.

**dual-motive conflict**: A conflict between two competing goals or motives.

**effect size**: A statistical index of the size of a particular difference between the things that are being studied.

**emergenesis**: Occurs when a trait is determined by a particular configuration of many genes that then leads a person to display a particular characteristic that is not seen in the rest of the person's family.

**eudaemonia**: The act of living one's life in a way that focuses on things that are intrinsically important for human well-being.

**evolutionary psychology**: A branch of psychology that focuses specifically on the evolutionary underpinnings of human behavior.

**explanatory gap**: The giant chasm between explaining how the brain works and explaining what produces consciousness.

**extroversion**: The degree to which people are talkative and sociable.

**flashbulb memory**: A very detailed, exceptionally vivid memory of the circumstances in which a person heard surprising, important, or emotionally arousing news.

**flow experience**: A psychological state that sometimes occurs when people are fully immersed in an activity.

**focalism**: The notion that when people think about how they will feel about some event in the future, they focus too much on the event itself and ignore all of the other things that will be going on that will influence their emotions.

**gene-environment correlation**: The effect in which genes affect people's environments.

**genotypic variance**: The variability in people's genes.

**grandiose narcissist**: A narcissist that evaluates himself or herself positively, as behavior seems to indicate.

**hedonic adaptation**: The tendency for people adjust to pleasurable changes in their circumstances so that something that initially brings happiness and pleasure usually wears off over time.

**heritability**: The proportion of the observed variability in a group of individuals that can be accounted for by genetic factors; the proportion of phenotypic variance that is attributable to genotypic variance.

**ideograph**: A character or symbol that represents an object or an idea.

**immediate-return environment**: An environment in which people can see the consequences of their behavior on an ongoing basis and receive immediate feedback regarding whether they are accomplishing essential life tasks.

**in-group favoritism**: Rating one's own group much more positively than another group.

**interdependence theory**: The relationship theory that states that each of us has a standard, called our comparison level, for judging whether we are making enough of a profit in our relationships with other people.

**interindividual-intergroup discontinuity effect**: The notion that groups of people are less cooperative and more competitive than individuals are.

**introversion**: The degree to which people are quiet and sometimes shy.

**Machiavellianism**: A personality characteristic that involves doing whatever it takes to get other people to do what you want, including being deceptive and dishonest and presenting images of oneself that are not accurate.

**mere ownership effect**: The notion that merely owning something makes people view it as better and more valuable.

**meta-analysis**: An analysis that statistically combines the results of many studies to reach a general conclusion.

**nature-nurture debate**: The debate over whether people's personalities are due mostly to nature—what they were born with—or mostly to nurture— how they were raised.

**neuroticism**: The degree to which people experience negative emotions.

**nightmare**: A dreams that is very vivid, involves strong negative emotions such as fear or grief, and wakes a person up.

**obsessive-compulsive disorder (OCD)**: A psychological disorder that involves the existence of uncontrollable thoughts, feelings, and ideas (obsession) that lead people to feel driven to engage in certain behaviors (compulsion).

**out-group homogeneity effect**: The tendency for people to think that members of groups other than their own are more similar to each other than they really are.

**oxytocin**: A hormone that promotes a feeling of social connection and of being bonded.

**parapsychology**: The field that studies anomalous psychic experiences such as extra-sensory perception (ESP).

**passionate love**: The kind of love that is intense and exciting at first and that usually involves sexual desire.

**personality**: Consistencies in a person's behavior across various situations and over time.

**phenotypic variance**: The variability that is observed in a trait or characteristic of people.

**phenylethylamine (PEA)**: A neurotransmitter that is related to amphetamines and whose effects on people's mood and energy are similar to those of various stimulants.

**precognition**: The awareness of some future event.

**presentiment**: The feeling of something that has not yet happened.

**psi**: Psychic phenomena.

**public self-consciousness**: A characteristic that describes the degree to which a person thinks about how he or she is viewed by other people.

**rapid eye movement (REM) sleep**: The stage of sleep that occurs once per cycle—and between four and six times per night—that is characterized by dreaming sleep.

**realistic conflict theory**: A theory that proposes that discrimination and conflict arise when groups are in competition for some scarce resource.

**relational value**: The amount of value that is placed on a relationship between people.

**risky behavior**: A behavior that has the potential to harm oneself or other people.

**Schadenfreude**: The pleasure that people experience over the misfortunes of another person.

**self-awareness**: The human ability to think consciously about oneself.

**self-compassion**: The degree to which people treat themselves in a kind and caring way when bad things happen.

**self-confidence**: The belief that you can do certain things or bring about certain outcomes.

**self-control strength**: The psychological energy it takes to make people do what they should and not do what they shouldn't.

**self-esteem**: How positively people feel about themselves.

**self-serving bias**: A bias that revolves around the notion that most people think that they are better than they actually are.

**serotonin**: A neurotransmitter that plays a part in the regulation of mood, sleep, learning, and other processes that involve the brain.

**shared influence**: An influence that is common to all children in a family.

**social anxiety**: The nervousness that people feel in social situations—such as on job interviews or on dates, when meeting new people, while being at a social gathering where they don't know anybody, or when speaking in front of groups.

**sociometer theory**: A theory that proposes that self-esteem is a gauge—an internal, psychological meter—that monitors the degree to which a person is being valued and accepted versus devalued and rejected by other people.

**state self-esteem**: A form of self-esteem that involves how you feel about yourself at any particular moment in time.

**subjective well-being**: An overriding sense of contentment and pleasure; a sense of well-being that goes deeper than happiness.

**subliminal stimulus**: A stimulus that cannot consciously be perceived.

**temporal discounting**: The notion that people discount outcomes that are further away in time.

**trace decay theory**: A theory that claims that a memory trace, which strengthens the connections in the brain that help to maintain a memory, is created every time a new memory is formed.

**trait self-esteem**: A form of self-esteem that reflects how good you feel about yourself in general or on average.

**unshared influence**: An influence that children in the same family don't share.

**vulnerable narcissist**: A narcissist that is fundamentally insecure about himself or herself.

# Bibliography

Baumeister, Roy F. *Is There Anything Good about Men?* New York: Oxford University Press, 2010. An engrossing, albeit controversial, examination of the question regarding why men display more personal and social problems than women.

Baumeister, Roy F., and John Tierney. *Willpower: Rediscovering the Greatest Human Strength.* New York: Penguin Press, 2011. A leading researcher reviews research on self-control in an accessible, applicable fashion.

Baumeister, Roy F., Jennifer Campbell, Joachim I. Krueger, and Kathleen D. Vohs. "Exploding the Self-Esteem Myth." *Scientific American* 292, no. 1 (2005): 84–91. A critical examination of the benefits and liabilities of self-esteem.

Blackmore, Susan. *Consciousness: An Introduction.* New York: Oxford University Press, 2004. An easy-to-read overview of what is known about consciousness.

Buss, David. *Evolutionary Psychology: The New Science of the Mind.* 4th ed. Boston: Pearson, 2011. An introduction to evolutionary psychology by one of the founders of the field.

D'Amato, Erik. "Mystery of Disgust." *Psychology Today* 31, no. 1 (1998): 40–49. http://www.psychologytoday.com/articles/200909/mystery-disgust. An examination of the evolved significance of disgust.

de Waal, Frans B. M. "The End of Nature versus Nurture." *Scientific American* 281, no. 6 (1999): 94–99. A noted primatologist explains why the nature-nurture debate is misplaced and should be laid to rest.

Eberhardt, Jennifer, and Susan T. Fiske, eds. *Confronting Racism: The Problem and the Response.* Thousand Oaks, CA: Sage, 1998. A collection of chapters by leading experts on prejudice and discrimination.

Eliot, Lise. *Pink Brain, Blue Brain: How Small Differences Grow into Troublesome Gaps—And What We Can Do about It.* New York: Houghton Mifflin Harcourt, 2009. A balanced, sometimes technical, examination of biological and social influences on differences between men and women.

Fisher, Helen E. *Why We Love: The Nature and Chemistry of Romantic Love.* New York: Henry Holt, 2004. A leading researcher reviews scientific research on the physiology of love.

Frank, Robert H. *Passions within Reason: The Strategic Role of the Emotions.* New York: W. W. Norton, 1988. A provocative and enjoyable book that explores the idea that emotions play an important, beneficial role in decision making and social interactions, even when they might seem to be irrational.

Goffman, Erving. *The Presentation of Self in Everyday Life.* New York: Doubleday, 1959. The classic introduction to the ways in which people manage their public images.

Harvey, John H., and Ann L. Weber. *Odyssey of the Heart: Close Relationships in the 21ˢᵗ Century.* Mahwah, NJ: Erlbaum, 2002. An introduction to research on close relationships—sprinkled with tidbits of advice.

Hassin, Ran R., James S. Uleman, and John A. Bargh, eds. *The New Unconscious.* New York: Oxford University Press, 2005. A collection of chapters on unconscious processes by leading scholars.

Higbee, Kenneth L. *Your Memory: How It Works and How to Improve It.* New York: Marlowe and Company, 2001. An accessible introduction to the psychology of memory with recommendations for improving it.

Hobson, J. Allan. *Dreaming: A Very Short Introduction.* New York: Oxford University Press, 2002. A concise look at research on sleep and dreams by a leading researcher.

Hock, Roger R. *Forty Studies That Changed Psychology*. 6<sup>th</sup> ed. New York: Prentice Hall, 2008. Examines some of the most important studies in psychological science, written in a casual and engaging style.

Horn, Stacy. *Unbelievable: Investigations into Ghosts, Poltergeists, Telepathy, and Other Unseen Phenomena, from the Duke Parapsychology Laboratory*. New York: HarperCollins, 2009. The history of scientific research on psychic phenomena with a focus on the groundbreaking work of J. B. Rhine.

Hyde, Janet S. "The Gender Similarities Hypothesis." *American Psychologist* 60, no. 6 (2005): 581–92. A review of research on gender differences—and similarities.

Krippner, Stanley, and Harris L. Friedman, eds. *Debating Psychic Experience: Human Potential or Human Illusion?* Santa Barbara, CA: Praeger, 2010. A collection of chapters debating the scientific evidence for psychic phenomena written by noted believers, debunkers, and skeptics.

Law, Bridget Murray. "Seared in Our Memories." *Monitor on Psychology* 42, no. 8 (2011): 60–65. An overview of cognitive psychological research on flashbulb memories.

Leary, Mark R. *Self-Presentation: Impression Management and Interpersonal Behavior*. Boulder, CO: Westview, 1996. Reviews research on why people are concerned with their public images and how self-presentational motives affect behavior and emotion.

———. "Sociometer Theory and the Pursuit of Relational Value: Getting to the Root of Self-Esteem." *European Review of Social Psychology* 16, no. 3 (2005): 75–111. A review of research supporting the idea that self-esteem is a gauge of social acceptance and rejection.

———. *The Curse of the Self: Self-Awareness, Egotism, and the Quality of Human Life*. New York: Oxford University Press, 2004. An exploration of personal and social problems that are caused by excessive self-awareness and egotism.

Leary, Mark R., T. W. Britt, W. D. Cutlip, and J. L. Templeton. "Social Blushing." *Psychological Bulletin* 112, no. 3 (1992): 446–460. A review of theory and research on blushing with a focus on the undesired social attention theory.

Lilienfeld, Scott O., Steven J. Lynn, John Ruscio, and Barry L. Beyerstein. *50 Great Myths of Popular Psychology.* Malden, MA: Wiley-Blackwell, 2010. An engaging look at 50 popular misconceptions about human behavior.

Lyubomirsky, Sonja. *The How of Happiness.* New York: Penguin Press, 2007. An international expert explains the effects of people's genetics, life situations, and behavior on happiness.

MacDonald, Geoff, and Mark R. Leary. "Why Does Social Exclusion Hurt? The Relationship between Social and Physical Pain." *Psychological Bulletin* 131, no. 2 (2005): 202–23. A review of scholarly research on hurt feelings.

Mauss, Iris. "Control Your Anger." *Scientific American Mind* 16, no. 4 (2005): 64–71. An insightful look at the catharsis hypothesis.

Miller, Rowland S. *Embarrassment: Poise and Peril in Social Life.* New York: Guilford Press, 1996. A leading researcher on embarrassment surveys research on this fascinating topic.

———. *Intimate Relationships.* 6th ed. New York: McGraw-Hill, 2012. A comprehensive overview of research on the psychology of close relationships, written in an engaging and accessible style.

Neff, Kristin. *Self-Compassion: Stop Beating Yourself Up and Leave Insecurity Behind.* New York: HarperCollins, 2011. An introduction to work on self-compassion with tips for increasing self-compassion.

Pawelski, Suzann Pileggi. "The Many Faces of Happiness." *Scientific American Mind* 22, no. 4 (2011): 50–55. An article-length review of scientific research on happiness.

Pinker, Steven. *How the Mind Works*. New York: Norton, 1997. A far-ranging survey of the ways in which evolution may have shaped human thought and behavior.

Reis, Harry, and Arthur Aron. "Love: What Is It, Why Does It Matter, and How Does It Operate?" *Perspectives on Psychological Science* 3, no. 1 (2008): 80–86. Two social psychologists provide a brief overview of what research has shown about the nature of love.

Rock, Andrea. *The Mind at Night: The New Science of How and Why We Dream.* New York: Basic Books, 2004. A nontechnical review of historical and contemporary research on sleep and dreaming.

Rutter, Michael. *Genes and Behavior: Nature-Nurture Interplay Explained.* Malden, MA: Blackwell, 2006. An introduction to the effects of genetic and environmental factors on both normal personality and psychological problems.

Sapolsky, Robert M. *Why Zebras Don't Get Ulcers.* New York: W. H. Freeman, 1996. An easy-to-read introduction to the psychology of stress.

Shaffer, David R. *Social and Personality Development.* 6th ed. Belmont, CA: Wadsworth Publishing, 2008. An introductory textbook that covers a wide variety of topics dealing with the myriad influences on people's personalities.

Sherif, Muzafer, O. J. Harvey, William R. Hood, Carolyn W. Sherif, and Jack White. *The Robbers Cave Experiment: Intergroup Conflict and Cooperation.* Middletown, CT: Wesleyan University Press, 1988. The original book-length report of the famous Robbers Cave study.

Steinberg, Laurence. *You and Your Adolescent: The Essential Guide for Ages 10–25.* New and rev. ed. New York: Simon & Schuster, 2011. An authority on how the brain changes during adolescence provides solid, research-based advice for parents and others who work with adolescents.

Tavris, Carol. *Anger: The Misunderstood Emotion.* New York: Touchstone, 1989. The classic book on the nature and functions of anger.

**Bibliography**

Twenge, Jean M., and W. Keith Campbell. *The Narcissism Epidemic: Living in the Age of Entitlement.* New York: Free Press, 2009. Two social psychologists present evidence that people are becoming increasingly self-absorbed and egotistical.

Walsh, David. *Why Do They Act That Way?: A Survival Guide to the Adolescent Brain for You and Your Teen.* New York: Free Press, 2004. An expert on child development explains why adolescents think and act differently than adults.

Westerhoff, Nikolas. "Set in Our Ways." *Scientific American Mind* 19, no. 6 (2008): 44–49. Discusses why people have greater difficulty changing themselves as they get older.

Williams, Kipling D. "The Pain of Exclusion." *Scientific American Mind* 21, no. 6 (2010): 30–37. The world's authority on ostracism describes the effects of social exclusion.

Wilson, Timothy D. *Strangers to Ourselves: Discovering the Adaptive Unconscious.* Cambridge, MA: Belknap Press, 2002. An engaging introduction to unconscious processes by a noted social psychologist.

Wright, Lawrence. *Twins: And What They Tell Us about Who We Are.* New York: John Wiley and Sons, 1997. A thought-provoking look at research on twins and what twin research tells us about the origins of personality.

# Notes

# Notes

# Notes

# Notes

# Notes